NEW MEXICO'S

Own

CLASSICAL GUITARIST

HECTOR PIMENTEL

NEW MEXICO'S *Own* CLASSICAL GUITARIST

HECTOR PIMENTEL

By Hector Pimentel

Edited by Robert Brent Gardner

Published by

Desert Wind Press

The events and conversations in this book have been set down to the best of the author's ability, although some names and details have been changed to protect the privacy of individuals.

Edited by Robert Brent Gardner,
Beverly Ledbetter and Rebecca Gardner
Cover Design by Hector Pimentel
and Robert Brent Gardner
Book Design by Robert Brent Gardner

Independently published by Desert Wind Press LLC
www.DesertWindPress.com

ISBN 978-1-956271-38-6 (print softcover)
ISBN 978-1-956271-39-3 (print hardcover)

Even though the guitar is a difficult instrument to play well, once you accomplish playing something you know, your guitar will be your friend for the rest of your life. It's your friend forever.

Once you touch the guitar, once you start playing it, it'll be right there. It's your friend.

Hector Pimentel

Table of Contents

Dedication 2

Inspiration 6

Music Education 16

Making a Name 22

On The Road 30

The Accident 40

Starting Over 46

Love and Music 52

Rick Pimentel 56

Robert Pimentel 60

Victor Pimentel 66

Pimentel & Sons Guitar Makers 70

Infania Pimentel 74

Rachael Pimentel 78

Robert Pimentel II 82

Jaime Pimentel 90

Javier Serecerez 96

William Loutfy 100

James Crabtree Sr. 104

Rick Ambrose 108

Ben Perea 114

Paul Benavidez 120

Richard Martinez 124

Victor Beserra 130

Family 138

Honors and Awards 146

Hector's Scrapbook 154

Fans, Fun and Celebrities 154

Discography 160

From the Publisher and Editor 166

Dedication

*I'd like to dedicate this book to my Mother and
Father, Josefina and Lorenzo Pimentel. They were,
and will always be, my inspiration.*

Inspiration

I remember my dad making guitars. We were very poor. My dad had a job as a baker and as a guitar maker. At first, he had his shop in the house, in our home. He would make guitars in the kitchen, while my mother finished cooking and all that. And then one day he asked me, "Son, can you help me with this? Just hold the soundboard." He didn't have very many tools, very few tools. So, here I am holding the soundboard on the kitchen table. He has no clamps. My fingers and my hands were the clamps. I was a little kid. I was maybe 8 years old, something like that. "Just hold it." He forgot to sand the edges of the soundboard, where it was cut around it. He pressed on the soundboard and guess what? It went into my thumb. I'm bleeding! That's when I knew, I don't want to be a guitar maker, ever.

About a year later, he said let's go see a concert. We saw Andres Segovia. One of the greatest guitarist ever. He was an old man then, he was very old. He was at Popejoy Hall, here in Albuquerque. I came inside the hall and I was listening to

everybody. I saw all these people, and I was looking everywhere. I was just a kid. I thought, wow, this is pretty cool. So we sat down and then the man came out, sat down, and then start playing the guitar. I was so impressed and so flabbergasted. I guess I was so surprised. I said, man, this man is playing so much music coming out of one guitar. Just one guitar. Oh my God! All classical music by Bach, Spanish composers, Francisco Tárrega, and Fernando Sor. All the famous composers in Spain for the classical guitar. And so I said to my dad during the intermission, "That's what I want to do, Dad. I want to do what he's playing. I want to be playing like him."

He said, "Are you serious?"

I said, "Yeah. Yeah, yeah."

That was a big turning point for my dad. I told him, "I don't want to be a guitar maker. You cut my fingers." So he said OK, alright. He got me into a class. Well, no, not at first.

There were a lot of people coming in to see my dad, guitar players, in our home. And so I would listen to his people playing. And there was this one doctor, Doctor Robert Foreman. He's still alive, and he gave me my first lesson, even though he wasn't a teacher, he was a doctor, a family doctor. I thought, man, this is pretty cool. That just playing one single note on the guitar. I said it sounds so cool. My dad made me a small guitar because I was little. And so I started taking lessons, and he hooked me up with a man by the name of Hector Garcia, who became one of my teachers. He was a concert artist. He was well known throughout the world and then he played here. He made his living here and toured throughout the United States. He became my teacher. I was like ten or eleven years old. He taught me until I was in my late 20s. So I took a lot of music from him. And during that period of time, I also took a lesson in jazz when I was in my early 20s from a jazz player named Bob Brown, a great jazz guitar player. He was a fantastic, great artist. So I had two teachers. Hector Garcia, my first teacher, though, didn't like the idea of me taking jazz lessons. But I had to tell him. He said it's going to ruin your technique as a classical guitarist. All right, well, you know now, so I kept quiet about that with him. I didn't want to talk to Hector Garcia about Bob Brown anymore

Young Hector, Age 18.

Hector's early fan club.

because I just wanted to learn from them both.

So my inspiration really came from my dad, my mom, and my brothers. My siblings and I were growing up, and I saw my mom and dad struggling so hard to make a living for us kids at that time.

I went to Albuquerque High School, and I graduated from there. When I was in school, I would take my guitar to school to practice because I was taking guitar lessons. I would practice and all the girls will come around and they would listen to me playing during lunch. Then I began to.get into a lot of fights with the guys who were playing sports because they got jealous of me. I would say, "Here we go again, another fight." And I said to my dad, "You better help me because I can't fight like that." But I did defend myself. I got into trouble because of that. From basketball players and. football players. I was in so much trouble. My dad used to take me out of school because I got into fights and told me he was called into the office and they said he has to take his son out of here because he gets into too much trouble. My son? Really?

So my dad would say, "Son, you can't be getting in trouble like that anymore."

"Well, I didn't start it. They did."

Another time, I was in Spanish class and this guy turns around and he messes with me. A big tall guy, a big football player. He pushed me. I said don't push me because he pushed me back. I'm a little tiny guy and he's a big, tall guy. He said, "I wanna meet you outside the school!" Oh great. Here we go. It was close to the last day of school. I told my brothers, hey, you better help me out because this guy I know, he's gonna bring a couple of other guys and he wants to mess me up. They asked, "So what happened now?"

"It's a guy in Spanish class that started trouble with me."

My brothers, they made machetes out of saw

Hector with his mother, Josefina, and father, Lorenzo.

blades and they wrapped them up with tape, just in case. They said, "Hector, you're always getting in trouble in high school."

"I didn't start it!"

So we put the weapons under the seat of the car. I went to the car and a bunch of guys were walking towards us. Oh, no. Here we go, I said. We see the guy from earlier that day. Rick gets out of the car and the rest of us get out of the car. We pull the machetes out and then they started taking off. And then Rick yells, "And you better not come back tomorrow! And if you do come, you better bring a gun!" I said "Rick!" I don't know what he was thinking.

That next day was the last day of school. We were in classes in the morning.and one guy in my class is saying "He's really gonna come after you today with people from other schools."

"What do you mean from other schools? Oh, you're just messing with me."

"No, I'm serious."

OK. So at that time we didn't have cell phones, but we went to the same school. So. I found my brothers in between classes. "Rick, Robert. They're going to come for me!"

They said, "Well, good luck, Hector. You're on your own buddy!" But then they said, "No, we'll be prepared. Don't worry."

Then we saw all these guys coming to the high school from everywhere. The guys had chains and knives. And I said, "Oh shit!" But a friend of mine who became a cop was there, and he said get inside my car because they're coming after you and they want to kill you and your brothers. I said, "Okay."

"Your brothers, they better get out of here, too."

So I'm in the back of this guy's car and he tells me to just hide down. Why am I doing this? "Because they're coming after you, Hector."

Oh, shit. All right. He was driving through school and kind of picked out guys with chains and knives who were looking for me. This friend says, "Just hide. Don't pick up your head because I'm going to take you home, alright?"

"And what about my brothers?"

"Don't worry about them. They'll be home too."

Anyway, so we all got home and everything was fine, but it was a scary moment for me.

I kept on going and that did not discourage me from playing my guitar. I loved the guitar so much that I didn't care about that. So I just kept on going. I got to meet, like I said, in the early days, a lot of people that would come and see my dad, from classical guitarists to flamenco players to jazz players to everything. I got exposed to all those people. And then my dad opened up his shop. He opened his shop in 1964 or 1965. But it was really smart. He bought this place, and it was a little house. He was working on it while he was still making guitars at home. He was working to make it into his shop. When in the 70s I was growing up and I was maybe 15 or 16 years old, I was listening to other people playing. I listened to his people playing. I was so impressed. In fact, Segovia was my first inspiration. That's what I wanted to do. So I got to meet other people, and I was learning from all these people just by watching them. Watching all these classical guitarists and I asked, how do you do that? I was just so curious. I was learning and wanted to know more and so I would ask them, can you teach me? Give me some exercises because I could see these people were so good at playing the guitar. I was always so impressed with these people.

I remember when he was making his guitars. He would be singing and playing some chords. And he was pretty good. He showed me a few chords when I was growing up. My dad would take me everywhere. I would go with him to the bakery where he made bread and all that.

He cut off one of his fingers in the bakery. It was his index finger. I remember when he cut it. We were very young when he cut his finger off and so when my dad got mad at us, we knew he was mad at us because he would point with his stub. "Come here!" We're in trouble! All my brothers. But we had a lot of respect for our parents in those days. I grew up in those days when there was a lot of respect for the parents. Parents knew how to be parents. They don't know how to be parents anymore. And my father was tiny. Imagine taking care of 13 of us. Imagine that whole army. Like I said, there was a lot of respect. We didn't have guns in our homes. Of course, we didn't have phones. We didn't have cell phones. I raised my kids almost the same way my dad taught us. That's why my daughter and my son and my young daughter, they're all doing really well. And they're well educated.

My father and my mom were from Mexico. And my cousins and my aunties were all from Juarez, Mexico. And so I went to visit my cousins from here in Albuquerque. I would go over and have fun there.

My uncle was dad's brother. He would come here and I would go to his house. I would see my auntie and my cousins, and my auntie would run to me as soon as I got there. "What you wanna eat? Whatever you wanna eat!" And I'd say, well, I don't know. I mean, I don't want to put you into any kind of trouble. "No, no, no. I'll get some steaks." So she would go to the store and get a fresh piece of meat and that's the way that it was. Because the grocery store was not very far from her house. So they would cook for me and then I'd play the guitar for them.

Guitars are the family. One time when I was a teenager, my father was taking some guitars because he was trying to sell his instrument. He wasn't very well known then. So, one day he took me along and we put a bunch of guitars in his car that he had just finished. I tagged along with him. We went to the store and of course, my father and I went inside the store and my father was talking business to the owner. I heard some commotion outside. Some guys were taking the guitars from the car. I think there were 3 or 4 guys, I can't remember. I yelled "Hey!" They started taking off, so I started running after them and there were cars in the parking lot and so they were running with the guitars, but they threw them under the cars. We got them all back, but some were broken. My father was trying to chase me down, not to go after these guys because he didn't know what was going to happen. I was young. I wasn't thinking about what could happen to me. I just wanted to get them back for my dad.

Once I started performing, I would play for my mom and dad and they'd look at me like they're very proud of me. My dad would drive the two of them to come see me. But my mom didn't drive. My dad never really wanted her to drive. He gave her the keys one time. She went so far and kind of wrecked the car, and that was the end of her driving career. My mother told my dad, "I need to get a license." He said, "But you only go from the kitchen to the bedroom. You don't need a license." That was my dad.

When I was learning how to play the guitar, my brothers were learning how to make guitars. So we're all in this little shop in my father's house. I'm playing and practicing and my brothers are working, sweeping the floor or whatever we're doing when we're young. We were all so young.

Our house was in northwest Albuquerque and my father made that into his shop because he didn't have a shop. The garage was his shop where he would cut the wood, and the basement is where he would spray the finish on the guitars. And as time went along, I was becoming a good student on guitar and, in my twenty's, I started going to different states with my father to sell my father's guitars.

I would ask my father to go with him and he would agree. He would send me with a bunch of guitars. We would go to California and sell guitars out there. We got orders from them and from Phoenix, Arizona. I went to a little college town out there, Tempe, and sold guitars to a classical guitarist who had a store and he would write me a check for the ones that I had and then he would put the orders. I did that for a while. My dad was very busy. I was traveling from state to state, maybe 3 or 4 states out here and even here in New Mexico. We would sell guitars to one particular store in Santa Fe called Candyman (Candyman String and Things). And I can remember the name of the person that owned it, but he was selling a lot of equipment. I even bought a stereo system from him. But, like I said, I was growing up and becoming an adult. I was traveling for my dad selling guitars because I played the guitar. I was really good at it in my early 20s. I would get my guitar from my dad that he made for me and I would go and try to solicit sales.

There was a period of time where it was kind of slow for my father. But there was this man who would come in, a folk singer. His name was Larry McGinnis, and he would buy tons of guitars from my dad. My dad would make the guitar cheap. I think they were going for $89.00 at that time. This guy wanted all the guitars and almost every two months or every month, he'd buy guitars for all his students. He had a lot of students doing the folk music, where people were singing folk songs. It must have been in the 70s.

I was demonstrating the guitar that way because I could play and people were impressed. At that time, there weren't a lot of classical guitarists around or classical guitar builders that were famous, like my dad. So, when people saw the instruments, they fell in love with them. The owners of the stores and such. But after a long time of him doing that, he stopped selling to stores and just started selling direct with custom guitars. But me and my brothers, we had a lot of fun. As they were learning guitar making, I was learning how to play guitar. We had a blast over here, laughing all the time and fighting sometimes. You were young and you're going to fight sometimes. But we love each other. We're family.

Victor, Lawrence, Hector, Rick, Lorenzo, Robert

Hector and Lorenzo Pimentel

Music Education

When I started my music education, when I was 11 or 12 years old, I started taking lessons from a person by the name of Robert Foreman, who was a doctor. The first book that I remember that I studied from was a Mel Bay book. I went through that for a couple of months and I knew a little bit of notes, because that's what Mr. Foreman taught. He taught me just a little because he didn't know very much either. He was just a rock'n'roll guitar player. I kind of was interested in how he played and I would ask him questions and he would show me. He was our primary doctor back then with my family. But he showed me and tried to teach me, but then he said, "You need to take lessons from a gentleman by the name of Hector Garcia." He was a concert artist and so I told my dad about him and he said they knew each other already. They knew each other because Hector Garcia and my dad came to Albuquerque about the same time, in the same year, I think, in the 1960s. They both came to Albuquerque and my father met Hector Garcia and they started talking about guitars and Mr. Garcia started asking my father about how he

made his classical guitars and he actually had some ideas of his own to give my dad. So they kind of worked together a little on that. Hector Garcia wanted a certain kind of sound. Because my father was not used to making classical guitars. I don't think he knew very much about classical music back then. My father was really pretty young, so he started educating himself more about that. After he took me to see Andres Segovia and I told him that's what I wanted to do, he started me with lessons from Hector Garcia and it was kind of great.

It was a good education for me because that's what I wanted to learn. I was amazed at what Mr. Garcia could do with a classical guitar. I just fell in love with the music and every note he played was so beautiful that he took me to another place. It was just such beautiful, gorgeous music. Spanish, classical, even Cuban music and Bach. I love Bach, some Mozart and Chopin, but mostly classical guitar. Fernando Soor, Ibanez Brasilia. So that's what I wanted to learn. The first book he started me on was by Emilio Pujol It was a very nice

Hector Garcia, world renowned concert guitarist and Hector Pimentel's teacher.

method. He went to study with one of his teachers, who was from Spain. He was gone for a couple of months and came back with a different kind of book. It was a guitarist from Spain and composer, Emilio Pujol, an educator in music. Mr. Garcia went almost every year to study with him. But then he would come back and share his ideas with me and his students that were taking lessons at that time.

I also took lessons from Bob Brown in Jazz so I could learn more about theory. He was a great musician. He was one of the greatest guitarists and in the world for me, because he never wanted to be famous. I asked Bob, "How come you don't want to go on and travel and make yourself more famous than what you are already?" "I don't want to do that," he tells me. "I just want to teach here and teach you." OK. So I learned. I took maybe six or seven years of guitar lesson from him. At the same time, I was also taking lessons from Mr. Hector Garcia. At the very beginning of when I first met Bob, I asked him, I'd love to take lessons from you. I was in my early 20s, and he said, "Well, I don't know what I can teach you. You're really good on the guitar." I said, "I want to learn and you can teach me a lot. I don't want to stop learning. I'd like for you to be my teacher." So he became my mentor. For about six years, something like that.

And after, we became really good friends, and we talked about jazz. We talked about classical music, we talked about flamenco music, and country music. He loved it all, too, but he was a great jazz guitarist. He liked to discover other salsa music. He was a great instructor. I learned so much from him. I learned theory and core progressions. I learned everything that I need to know to arrange music as well. Classical instructors don't really take you through theory. They're readers. That's what we do. We read and that's how we do our music for the most part. That's it.

Whether it was jazz, classical, in style music, I like it all. You know, I'm not too much into flamenco. I like the style. I don't like it as much, like Andre Segovia. He never liked flamenco, ever, and I was in the same boat. I enjoy listening to a couple of pieces and that's about it. So I played it but I played that kind of music that wasn't traditional because it wasn't, well, flamenco. And I don't call myself a flamenco player because I'm not.

Bob Brown was a great innovator. He was an innovator in jazz, and he also played classical music and he was really good at classical guitar, too. But he would ask me questions about classical music. He knew I was a classical guitarist, so he wanted to know more. And we kind of went back and forth. It wasn't that I taught him because he was a great instructor, a great teacher, but I just gave some of my ideas and then would put it his way. For example, he wanted to find out about certain people as Jesu, Joy Of Man's Desiring by Bach. And he asked me, "what do you think about this Hector?" And I said that's very nice. That's different from how most classical guitarists would play it, but that sounds really great. It's beautiful. And he arranged that. He knew how to arrange music. That's what I wanted to do. I wanted to do what he did.

One thing that I learned and I teach my students is you should learn the technique of the instrument. The classical guitar technique. That's pretty straightforward, but we teach you certain positions with your hands and how to hold the guitar. To be perfect with the guitar.

In the late 70s and early 80s, I started studying extensively guitar. There were a lot of students that I used to go to visit at the University of New Mexico. I used to hang out and see all the other guitar players there were taking lessons from Mr. Garcia. I wasn't a student at UNM. I just went out there and visited. I made a lot of guitar friends. There was this one girl that I was kind of chasing, Barbara Tupoy, a beautiful Spanish girl. And of course, she never gave me the time of day, but well, actually, we were friends, but she didn't go out with me. So I tried, but she played the guitar beautifully, too. She was ahead of me by about a year in her studies.

Like I said, I used to hang around with those people just to learn from them, and I was watching. It was interesting to me because there were students like me and some were extremely good. Better than I would have ever been. But you know you just learn from these people. I would go to guitar concerts almost every year, there at Keller Hall or Popejoy Hall, going to just learn. They'd always have famous guitar players coming in from different parts of the United States and even Spain. It was terrific. I'm sure they still do it. I know they have a guitar department out there and one of the professors was one of my students, Benjamin Silva.

Hector Garcia was a professor there, and he didn't want to do it anymore, so he quit teaching and retired from UNM. He taught privately, so I continued taking lessons from him until he passed away, which was four years ago. I used to ask him a lot of questions.

Then there was another professor that came to UNM. His name was Michael Chapdelaine, and he was kind of arrogant. He came in the 90s. When he came into the picture, I wanted to meet him. I wanted to show him one of my dad's guitars. I didn't know the kind of person he was, so I went to UNM and I met him. I said I'm a guitarist and my family are guitar makers. He said he'd heard of them. I said, so here's one of them. At that time in the 90s, I was playing popular music, and I started

playing Send In The Clowns. I wasn't trying to say something nasty about a clown, but he said, "I don't like that kind of music." OK. But you know, I think it was the song. Maybe he thought I was making fun of him, but I wasn't. I just wanted to show him how the guitar sounded. So he took the guitar and started playing beautiful music. But then he said, "I don't play pop music and I don't like pop music." OK, well, fine. I just came here to play something just to show him how the guitar sounded and I didn't argue with him. I just said thank you and nice meeting you.

Later, I would be playing around town, for example, for the holidays, I would play at Dillard's for Christmas music. They would hire me to do that. They don't do that anymore, unfortunately. So here I am playing my Christmas music and I see Michael Chapdelaine coming down the stairway. And then I say OK, I'll play some more popular music and some classical but more of the popular. And then he would just follow me, like a stalker. A guitarist stalking another guitarist. So I would see him at a restaurant just kind of sneaking around. And about three years later, he started playing popular music! After all that! That's a true story. That's a fact. I don't care what anybody says, that's why he started playing popular music. Because of me.

They say you make more money playing popular music than you do playing classical music. And you hardly ever see anyone playing classical music in town. People don't get it. Every now and then, it's nice to play a classical piece. They like it, but if you do that throughout the whole set, they don't like it.

Michael Chapdelaine played in front of Segovia. I saw a video. Segovia had master classes and here are all these classical guitar players. He comes to Michael Chapdelaine, who was very young. He started playing something and Segovia says go tune your guitar. Tune your guitar and get out of here. When you come back with your guitar in tune, then you can play some more. So he came back the same day, and he started playing something by Bach. Segovia looked at him and said, "Why are you doing it that way?" He just tore him up. "Why are you not doing it my way? Why are you not doing it the way I'm playing it?" Michael Chapdelaine couldn't even say, and so that was the end of his performance with Segovia.

So, taking lessons from Hector Garcia, I started the Emilio Pujol books. I went through four of his books. The extensive study and their ideas from scales to arpeggios to short studies and pieces that I had to perform as well and for the recitals that I had to do. But I went through extensive study. I love finger exercises that I went through and they didn't take one year. They didn't take two years. It was five or six years of extensive study. Like a doctor or others that go through all that. Your

primary basic training that goes for years. I studied with Hector Garcia for 20 years or so, maybe more. I was just studying and studying.

Young Hector with classical guitarist Hector Garcia.

Making a Name

So as time went along, I started promoting myself in my early 20s. I did that because I wanted more work, and I didn't think about getting famous or anything like that. I just wanted to get more work for myself.

What I would do, I would start making posters, hanging posters all over the city. I had to run around the city because at that time we didn't have cell phones, computers, or the Internet.

Back in the early days, to promote myself, I would go to radio stations that played classical music. They would interview me. I was a young man. Here, I'm getting interviewed and, of course, my English was even worse then than it is now. Spanish was my first language.

When I was between 17 and 18 years, I got my first gig playing guitar and all classical music in a little restaurant here in Albuquerque. I was playing my guitar, and I was a teenager looking at all the pretty girls. I thought, this is going to be fun.

I moved out of my home when I was 18 years old. I moved out of there as soon as I got out of high school. I got inspired by not only the music but also the people that were listening to me that I enjoyed playing for, sharing what I had in talent at that time.

I kept on going and then when I was 21 years old, I got my first gig at a hotel restaurant near the airport. I got to meet a lot of famous people. There were a lot of people that came into the restaurant there. I met Ricky Nelson. He was eating dinner, and he liked what I did. It was all classical and while he wasn't into that, he enjoyed it. We talked very little. It was very brief. He was there and having dinner with some people. And he had his guitar with him. And of course, everybody knew who he was, but I didn't know who he was. But, hey, OK.

And then one day when I was playing in the restaurant and while all these famous people were coming in, there was one guy. He was a union member or a union president or something. And he said his name was Prince Bobby Jack. I don't know who this guy was. He looked at me, he goes, "You can't play here. You can't play music here."

I said, "What's that? And who are you ?" Here

Prince Bobby Jack

we go again, I thought, another fight.

He says, "My name is Prince Bobby Jack and I'm the president of the union. And you're not supposed to be playing here. Unless you're a union member."

"Why don't you talk to the manager because you can't be talking to me like that?"

And he got really mad, and he goes, "Yes, I can". He had a gun, and he showed me the pistol.

"What are you going to do with that? Why did you show it to me? I don't want to see that." I said, "Well, where's the manager? You're the one that came marching in and telling me off and I can't be playing here. Come on, get out of here." So he took off.

The only thing that came out of that was apparently these people, the hotel, had to join BMI so they can have music there. The managers told me, don't worry about, we'll take care of that.

You don't have to worry about this guy and, yeah, we know who he is. He said he's a troublemaker. So he just wants money from musicians like you. But the union wasn't very strong. If you're in LA or Chicago, maybe, but not here in New Mexico.

I got to meet other actors, as well. They would stay at the hotel because they would be making a movie in town. Like James Caan. Let me tell you a story about that guy. Here, I'm playing at the hotel, and he comes barging in like the other guy. "You can't be playing. The music is going into our movie" and you've got to stop playing here in the restaurant. There were people there that wanted to hear me play for a wedding they were going to have at the hotel. I said, "You just can't be doing that, sir."

"Yes, I can." James Caan is the same way you see him in movies. That's the way he is in person. He went off on me and he came with an entourage of people. So here I am. James Caan comes in and again, I didn't know who this man was.

"You're interrupting the movie," he says.

I said, "Do you have a contract with the movie producers? Do you have a contract with them?"

"Yeah, I do."

"And so do I. I have a contract with a manager here. You cannot tell me to stop playing."

"Is that so? I want to talk to your manager. Where is he?"

"Oh, he's in LA right now. Where are you

from?"

And then the security came, and the cops came and threw him out. And the next day he was in the newspaper that he had a fight with me and they didn't mention my name because he didn't know

who I was. He said, "I got into a fight with this guitar player. I'm a rodeo rider and I'm a this and a that, a boxer." Even the newspaper made-up what he said of himself. After that. I didn't like him. I didn't want to see him. I didn't watch any of his movies.

As people heard me, I started getting more gigs. I played weddings and then in 1988, they had a big festival of guitar players in Santa Fe. One player was Ottmar Liebert. He became a really famous guitar player from Santa Fe. So here I am in 1988. There were maybe about 15 guitar players all through the whole day. My turn was next, and then Ottmar Liebert, I think before or after me, anyway. So I heard Ottmar Liebert playing classical guitar. I thought, he's OK. I mean, not a big deal. There were other people that were a lot better. And here I am. I play my music and then he played.

I heard some other great guitar players, and they're all good. A year later, I hear about Ottmar Liebert. I didn't think he was that good. But all of a sudden I started hearing about him. I thought, he's pretty good. He became really famous for playing flamenco, salsa, those kinds of songs. And I said, wow, I can't believe he did that. So I said OK, well, if he's going to do that, I'm going to do that too. I started my band because of him and the Gypsy Kings.

I was playing all classical music. No popular music. So people would ask me, can you play this? Can you play that in pop music? I started thinking to myself, the more people ask me for pop music, the more I got interested in trying to learn that style.

I put my group together, and I did some

Ambrose Rivera, Hector, Yolanda Lange (Little Anita's, Candelaria & Rio Grande)

arrangements of Ottmar Liebert music and some of Gypsy Kings too, for the whole group. The group had 5 people and sometimes other people would join us. I had me on the guitar. I also had a rhythm guitar, bass guitar, congas, castanets, and dancers. I changed members every now and then because someone would want to go their own way. But I kept most of my members together for a long time. When we played together, we went all over. We went to San Bernardino, California, and Las Vegas, Nevada. We went to Winnipeg and Alberta, Canada. I played in Japan with my flamenco band. The band's name was Hector Pimentel and Leyenda. We were getting famous.

I was playing restaurants, political parties, events. And at that time, there were very few guitarists that were performing. I was probably one of the very few, one or two, of the very few performers. Everybody just wanted to be a concert artist. I mean, all the people that were taking guitar lessons. That's what they were going for, including me. But, I think back, I couldn't wait to make money and perform for people and enjoy myself. That's why the classical artists would criticize me. Oh, you're playing in a restaurant? Why are you doing that? Because I like it and I enjoy it. And why are you playing a club? Oh, come on. Also, classical guitar players don't use amplifiers, including flamenco players, too. They're very traditional. I got away from that. The reason that I got away from that was because I heard Chet Atkins, and I thought he was great. And when I first heard him play, he was playing this beautiful pop music. I never heard it before because I was all stuck in classical music and I said, wow, this is

beautiful. This finger style, classical style. In fact, Chet Atkins took classes from Andres Segovia and they were both famous. Wow! They were both famous. So you keep on learning. I'm still learning at this time of my life. I still keep learning from other people. You never stop.

So I started thinking about the people that were asking me for pop music. I said, well, this is my time, and I started listening to it and decided I'm gonna start doing that. So I started taking jazz lessons to try to arrange music because there were no arrangements for pop music for classical guitar. Yeah, a lot of classical music, but you don't have any pop music. Not back then. So I started doing arrangements like this. This is a song I'm getting ready for Christmas. "It's the Most Wonderful Time of the Year." It's a beautiful song. And then I do things like "The Entertainer" and "If I Were a Rich Man." People keep asking me for that.

I started reading music at a very early age. I started learning how to read music when I was like nine years old or ten years old, when I started taking lessons. I learned how to read and learn how to move my little fingers because I was just small. I see a lot of my kids, some of my students are children, and I see their little fingers moving all over. And that reminds me of myself when I was growing up. It reminds me of my childhood.

I've had so many students throughout my life because I started teaching and had my first student at 19 years old. At nineteen years old, I started teaching guitar. So a long time. And ever since then I've been teaching and playing guitar.

Over time, I got to meet some very famous people, sculpture artists and other artists at events I did. I got to meet a lot of great politicians. I started getting hired by political people for the Republicans or Democrats. I didn't know anything about that and I didn't care. And I still don't care. They would hire me to play for Bruce King, the governor, Jerry Apodaca and all those people that were here as I was growing up. I got to meet all these political people because of my music. I played for John Kerry and John Edwards when they were running for president. I played for the president of the State Bar association, Jay Brent Moore. I played an event for Judy Nakamura, when she became the Chief Justice of the New Mexico Supreme Court, hosted by the Govenor Susana Martinez.

Carol and Hector with
Susana Martinez, former Governor of New Mexico

Judy Nakamura, Chief Justice of the NM Supreme Court
with Hector

Hector with President Bill Clinton

Spanish Classical Guitarist

"In addition to being at one with his audience, he is also at one with his guitar."

— *Ralph Andrews, Ph. D., San Bernardino Times*

Hector Pimentel

New Mexico's own "Mr. Guitar"

Pimentel & Sons

Guitar Makers, Inc. - Music & Entertainment

Contact: Rick or Robert (505) 907-6668

3316 Lafayette Dr. N.E. - Albuquerque, NM 87107

On The Road

When I first started performing with my band, it was in 1990. We started performing out-of-state, getting some concerts together. In the band, I was the lead guitarist. The members of Leyenda were Yolanda Lang on percussion and castanets. She was also a flamenco dancer. Ambrose "Sonny" Quilban was rhythm guitar. He left the band and Ernesto Quilban, his brother, took over. Ray Avila played electric bass. Victor Beserra played bongos. Matthew Vaughn on violin at one time. And Amy O'Brien from Santa Fe, who played the oboe. She recorded on one of my albums. I love the oboe. It was a great moment to play the guitar with her.

In 1992, we went to California. We played Santa Monica and San Bernardino. That's where we started with the first big performance that we did.

In San Bernardino, in the amphitheater, we were playing for a big audience one evening. We were playing mostly neuvo flamenco music, but I was getting a little bored and I said let's do "Dust In The Wind" by Kansas. My whole band thought I was kidding. But I said, "Come on. We know this." So we started, and the crowd loved it. They held up their lighters and were waving them back and forth. They loved it because it was different.

And then we went to the Henderson Amphitheater in Las Vegas and played there. We also played in Scottsdale, Arizona, at a resort. It was a nice outside venue with water misters, so it was nice and cool.

Later on, I played nightclubs in New York and Chicago. I was in New York about a month, playing guitar at a jazz club. I would find other guitar players or bass players to do the gigs. I would investigate who was around and was good. Other times, we'll bring some of the members of my band and take them to New York and play out there. And it was fun. And not only that, but we went all over the Broadway area in New York and to check out different music. So we did that for a number of years until 2001, before we were attacked. It was in August 2001, the last time I was there.

We played Japan in the early 1990s. We played in Sasebo, Kyoto and Osaka. Japan was really interesting to me. The people were so nice and I thought I was tiny, but they were tinier. I'm 5-6 and I felt like a giant to these people. We played nuevo flamenco, not traditional flamenco. I like to emphasize that because I don't want people to think I'm a flamenco player because I'm not. The Japanese people loved it. They loved it so much that the next day they showed us their style of flamenco. It didn't sound like flamenco, but anyway, it was interesting how they interpreted it.

We played in Houston in an amphitheater out there at a festival. It was in July and it was a big festival where they had different groups. They were all famous except for my group. They were all playing R&B, rock'n'roll and we're playing neuvo flamenco. We got there in the morning and it was so hot and humid. But I didn't think anything of it until a couple of hours later. I said this can just stick it out. This park was huge, and they had built a big stage.

So we went on about 3 o'clock in the afternoon and we're all sweaty. Remember, we've been there since the morning and it was raining. It would start raining and then it was so hot. I mean, it was just horrible. It was our turn to get up on stage. "OK, you guys are on." Alright, let's go. So we went out there and we had posters of myself and my group and we were throwing the posters to the audience and the people were grabbing them and screaming. We are doing our thing and the people there were getting into our music. It was crazy. And finally, we did our last song. So we got off the

back of the stage and our limo came in. We could not all fit in it, so I said, "You guys go ahead. I'll stick around. Don't worry about it. I know you guys are tired." I was tired, too, and sweating. They took off and then a bunch of girls came in, all beautiful Spanish women. And they said, "Let's go take a picture with you." "You sure?" "Yeah, yeah" I forgot that I was sweating and I was tired, but I didn't think of that anymore. I was just around these beautiful girls. I got pictures of that. I actually went out with one of them that night.

So my limo came. It was a big old Hummer. "Your limo was here, Mr. Pimentel." OK, so I knocked on the door and a big black guy comes out. I thought, "Oh, sh*t, what did I do?"

I said, "I'm sorry, man, but I'm tired. I just want to get back to the hotel." He said, "We get it, but don't worry. Hey, you're that musician, the guitarist. Yeah, we get it. We're tired too. But we're going to perform now." I said, "Well, I'm sorry. I'm not going to hang out here." I was just desperate to get in that limo.

Then a bunch of black guys get out of the limo and last, a white guy comes out. He asks me, "You don't know who these guys are?" I knew he was going to be mad because I said, "No, I don't and I don't care. I just want to go back to my hotel room." I didn't know who these people were, and I said I don't care who they are. I did my thing. So I got in the limo and I fell asleep for a little bit. I got

Lyenda band members (front) Victor Beserra, Ernesto Quilban, Ray Avila, (back) Yolanda Lange and Hector Pimentel.

to my hotel room and I walked out into the hall and saw my band members. I asked, "So who the hell are Boys To Men?" and I told them about the guys in the limo. "Are you serious?" they asked. "Yeah, I'm serious. I don't know who they are." "They're a famous R&B group, Hector! Come on!" Well, I didn't listen to that style of music. But I started to after that, and I thought these guys were good.

Here in Albuquerque in the1990's, we started playing the Hilton, now the Crowne Plaza. We played there for 12 years, every Friday night. Four nights of playing solo and the other night I was playing with my group. That place was so packed with people on Friday nights. The people there, all the audience and everybody were having fun, including us. We were all having fun. And at that time, they had all you could eat chicken fajitas, beef fajitas, and all the beer you could drink, so people got crazy. But it was a lot of fun, though, until the last two years. They started having flights, so they had to stop. They had to stop the performances, unfortunately. Some bad apples in there and it ruins everything, you know.

During one of my performances at the Hilton Hotel, we had a lot of people from universities and out of town. So we're getting into playing this music and we're playing, I think it was Malaguena. I did a beautiful arrangement of that. Everybody loved it. In fact, I won an award for that

Hector and Victor Beserra (congas) and Wayne Reynolds (bass) performance Hispanic Cultural Center ABQ

Hector Pimentel

Amina Lozada, Hector, Ricardo Pachenco

Crystal Zamora and Hector.

arrangement. Anyway, we're really into playing the music and all of a sudden when I was strumming, not trilling, and I was doing the scales on the guitar, my fingernail got caught in one of the strings and it just broke my nail along with a pick on top of it and it went flying. And here I am still continuing to play while my finger was bleeding. So we had to stop because I was hurting and so I asked my band to stop. We finished the song and then people started applauding. During the applause, I asked my dancer, Yolanda, if she saw my fingernail flying off because I saw it go by her. She goes, "Yeah, I saw it, Hector." I asked her, can you go grab it? Can you can you find it? So she was looking desperately for it and she found it. While that was happening, my fingernail was bleeding, my hand full of blood. So I said guys,."Well, let's take a good break and I've got to fix my nail." So I went to the curio shop at the hotel and I asked for some super glue. I'm hurting and blood everywhere. So the clerk sold it to me. I prayed to God that I was going to be OK. I opened the bottle and put it on my finger so I could put my fingernail back together again and it burned the heck out of me. It was burning so badly and there was a lot of pain. Not that I wasn't in pain already, but the super glue made it worse. It was burning so badly I had to go to the bar and ask for a double shot of tequila so the pain would subside. It didn't help, but I had to do what I had to do. I had to use

different fingers so I could continue playing the rest of the night. You adapt. I had to. That's what we, as well as all musicians, do. We gotta do what we gotta do to continue doing our performing.

But one of the most important things that we

did here in Albuquerque with my band was we played at the zoo. We did concerts there for five years. We'd play at the zoo amphitheater. It was really nice because they have a little pond and the stage on the other side. People would sit down and listen to our music. I mean, tons of people. Those

were fun times, from 1993 to 1998, for five years.

After that, they start hiring other musicians from out of town. But that was OK, you know, because we did our thing and we enjoyed it and we filled the amphitheater. That was a lot of fun. We had a blast.

I was asked to play for two generals at Kirtland Air Force Base. One was a dinner party for General Wise, a two-star general. He really loved my music. I can't remember if he'd heard me before, but he really enjoyed what I did.

And then right after that, I think it was a four-star general that came to Albuquerque and they asked me to play for him, General Randolph.

Those were quite interesting performances because I really, really enjoyed being around people like that. I was just overwhelmed playing for them.

I also played for an actor, Edward James Olmos, a couple of times for screenings of his films here in Albuquerque. Once for "Caught" and "Selena".

When I was younger, I played background music for a reading of "Bless Me, Ultima", read by the author, Rudolfo Anaya. It was at Albuquerque University, now, St. Pius High School. I was 17, I think.

I'd also do brunches for Easter Sunday and Mother's Day here in Albuquerque. It was one of my favorite times to do performances. Weather permitting, at the Hyatt or the Hilton.

I used to play Delfino's at the Four Seasons

Motor Inn here on Carlisle five nights of the week, and I lasted there a long time. They also had the Crystal Room in the main building. It was a fine dining room with the best steaks and everything. I never ate in there, but I used to peek in there. I was just a kid, but I was curious about everything. So they had a piano player playing there and they have me on the other side playing guitar. I was getting more well known, and I had my group. And so I was doing more stuff and more concerts, high-end restaurants, that kind of thing. So I was very busy. Incredibly busy.

In December of 2001, after 9-11, there was an event for first responders at the Isleta Casino that they asked me to play. They wanted patriotic music, so I played God Bless America, The Star-Spangled Banner, Amazing Grace, and America the Beautiful. I did my own arrangements of those for it.

I was pretty booked, and I was playing all the time and on top of that, I had 60 students. I was teaching here in the shop. So my other true love is teaching guitar. I love giving instructions and I've had a lot of good students. In fact, one of my students is now a professor at UNM, Benjamin Silva. And then I have another one at The Albuquerque Academy, Jeremy Mayne. I think he teaches guitar out there, so I have students there.

So you pass your talents and you pass your knowledge to your students and to the public. You know, for the love of your music and what you want to share with everybody, and that includes my students. My students expect that.

Lyenda members Hector Pimentel, Victor Beserra, Yolanda Lange, Mike Swick and Ambrose "Sunny" Rivera

The Accident

One day my dad said, guess who was here? Ottmar Liebert. Oh, that guy? He bought a guitar from my dad here after he became famous. But I never got to meet him when he was here, because I was traveling or whatever I was doing. But I respect him because he did what he did and became famous with the guitar and, of course, exposed classical guitar to more people, which I wasn't able to do until after he became famous. Now I was getting famous too. And then as time went on, my career was going up and up until 2005 when my accident happened

We were playing an event at the University of New Mexico, and we had the Hilton later that night. We were playing from 5:00pm to 7:00pm for President Caldera at the time. It was Friday. May the 13th of 2005. We're performing. The people there asked, do you want a little glass of wine? No, I don't drink wine. But, they gave me a little glass. So not bad. So we continued playing and then 7:00 came along and we finished. The President thanked me and the band. As we're packing, the security guard asked us to close the loading dock gate, where we were parked next to the Zimmerman library. It was at the Zimmerman Library where we were playing for president, and next door was a loading dock. That's where all the trucks go in and whatever they do, so we're parked in there, because that's where they asked us to park. So the security guy asked can you do me a favor and close the gate for me and I say, yeah, I'll do it. I told my guys, go ahead and go to the Hilton and I'll be there in a few minutes. They said, OK, we'll go set up for you. I'll just close the gate myself. So I drove my car from the loading dock after putting my guitar inside and everything. I went back to the gate, and I got the gate to almost close. As I was closing it, it dropped on me. It was a freak accident. The gate hit the curb, and that's all the space I had from being crushed. I was bleeding everywhere, but not knowing that I was bleeding, not knowing that I was badly hurt. And so I was screaming for help to get me out of here. I was like a pancake. And it was still light, since it was May. And all these people came and lifted up the gate. They pulled me out of there. I was sitting down under a tree and holding onto my nose because it was ripped off. I still have a scar. So I was waiting and waiting, but I didn't know what I was waiting for.

Then the paramedics, police, and a fire truck came. I could remember the tree in front of me, that leaves were real calm. And here, I'm under the tree, and I still can see. Then the paramedics came up.

"We want to see you," they said.

"Oh well. I'm OK. I'm fine. I just wanna go home."

They looked at me. Really? This guy's delirious. And they said, "OK, we're going to pick you up."

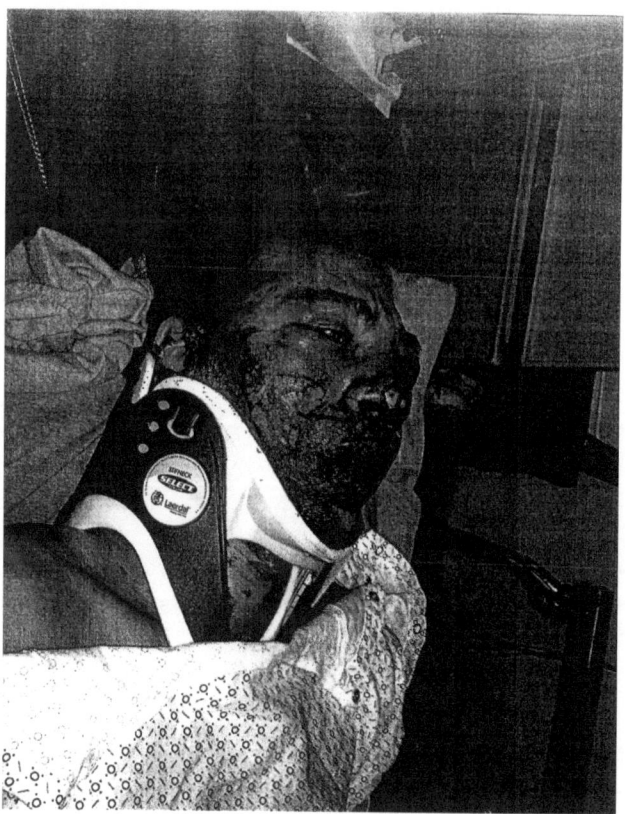

So they pick me up and I fainted. I was in no pain at all whatsoever. Nothing. No pain and blood everywhere. But I didn't even know there was blood. They put me on a gurney. I came to briefly and then just shut off. Then I was inside the ambulance and here I was with the paramedics, talking. And I was awake.

They asked, "Mr. Pimentel, have you been using recreational drugs, or have you been drinking?"

"No, I don't do any of that. And well, I did have a little glass of wine, but it was just a little tiny glass. I don't even like wine."

Here, I'm talking to the paramedics like that. Then the paramedics said, "We're gonna cut your suit off."

"Oh, you can't do that. You can't. That's an expensive suit. I just bought it. It cost me $800."

"Well, Mr. Pimentel, it's ripped."

"I don't care."

Yeah, so, I'm in the ambulance and they started taking the shoes off and I go out. I didn't see anything anymore. I guess I must have been getting bloated like that. So I ended up in the ER and then I hear voices and, not that I'm crazy, but I couldn't see. I couldn't see, but I was still in no pain. I thought I was still fine. And I remember saying I need water. I need water. Oh, we can't give you water. And then I heard somebody say "Is this guy gonna make it?" and "I don't think so." I thought, I hope they're not talking about me. Then

I said I need water and don't let the paparazzi in here. One of the guys in the ER lost it when I said that.

After that, somebody put a piece of ice on my mouth and I was gone. I don't know how long I was in the hospital. I started opening my eyes, and they said they were going to do plastic surgery on me. I said wow, plastic surgery. OK, can you may look like Antonio Banderas? And I was still joking, but then I was on morphine. I had all kinds of tubes in me.

I was feeling good. Even with broken bones. I got broken bones in my face and broken teeth and broken arm, broken ribs, broken pelvis. I had a traumatic brain injury on top of it all. I couldn't remember anything. They said they were going to put this thing in you. There was a big tube. I remember seeing that tube. I said no. That's not going to happen. The doctor said, "Oh, we have to do that. And besides, we numb your throat. We know that's going to help. And I'll tell you what I'm going to do." It's a camera that they use so they

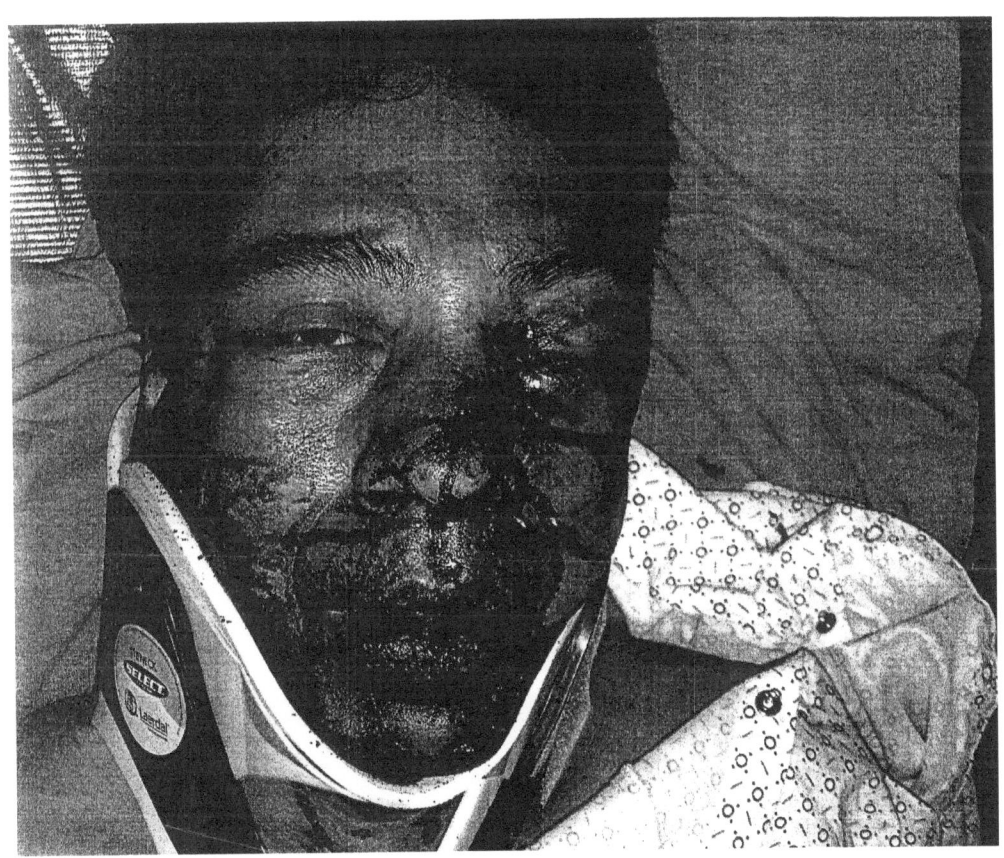

can see inside you. I guess that's what it was for.

Yeah, they put me out. I was out, and they did the surgery and they put in plates. I've got plates in my cheeks, my head, my jaw. And of course, 14 or 15 teeth were shattered. But that titanium teeth thing happened almost a year and a half or two years later. The teeth that were there were shattered, with some of the bones stuck in my gums. So they had to take everything out. That was a long process. I was in the hospital about a month and two weeks.

When I was in the hospital, some of my students came to see me. I love my students because they knew. They heard in the news that I was injured real badly and some people were surprised that I was alive. They thought that I had passed away, and they didn't know that I was still alive.

After I got out of the hospital, I wasn't able to walk and I was in a wheelchair. I started picking up the guitar eight months later. I started trying to move my fingers after I started. So I was playing. Then I started taking lessons again from Mr. Garcia, because he knew that I was badly injured, so he helped me along the way. One day, my ex-wife took me down to the Hilton to see everybody. Reluctantly, but she took me down there and I got to see everybody like the security guard and the staff, people that I knew really well. They were pretty sad because I was so I'm banged up and I was in a wheelchair. I knew that they were feeling bad for me, but I wanted to be there. And I wanted to be part of what I used to be, because, I mean, twelve years of playing at the Hilton. Yeah, I knew a lot of people. They were compassionate.

It took me a long time to recover. It took me a couple of years from 2005 until the end of 2007.

"You know, sometimes it is the artist's task to find out how much music you can still make with what you have left."

Itzhak Perlman

Starting Over

In 2007, I got a call from Hollywood and they said, "Mr. Pimentel, we got your CD's here. We heard really good things about you. We want you in a movie."

I said OK. I was thinking to myself, I don't know about this.

"Mr. Pimentel, we really like your music. We've got your CDs. It's just gonna be for one day. We want four songs. So if you don't mind, how much do you think you will charge us?"

Hollywood, huh? So I say, "Seven thousand."

"OK. Well, we'll send you a check right away."

I thought this was a scam at that time. I don't think it's true, but OK. So a few days later I got a check and the instructions and everything that I had to do. I had to go out to the Botanical Garden where they have the restaurant. They made it look like what you saw in the movie, "Bordertown".

I don't really know how they got my CDs. Up until at that time, in the 90s up to the 2000s, people wanted CDs from me like crazy. I recorded six CDs. The people would come to the hotel at the Hilton Hotel for years from 1990 until 2002 or 2003. I was there for a long time and was, apart from doing my concerts and all that, I was playing there five nights out of the week at the Hilton. I mean, things were good for me. I also had students. I was playing Wednesday through Sundays the whole time. And on Fridays, I had my band. It was so crazy. I was there for 12 years. And so every Friday, I mean during the week, it was kind of busy, but Friday was jam-packed because they have fajitas and they have my band. In fact, I just saw a thing on Facebook where they asked what restaurants or what clubs were the most fun, and one of the ones they mentioned was one guy mentioned he loved seeing Hector. I saw that I said to myself, wow, people remember me from back in the day.

At the end of 2007, that's when I met my wife, Carol.

Carol: We met at Sandia Casino. I went after a service at Calvary Chapel and I saw a girl that I went to church with up at the front and I said I'm going to go stand with Sharon and cut in because it was a big long line. So I went and stood with Sharon and Hector and his sister were there in the little group. Hector comes up to me and looks at my necklace and he says, "How far does that necklace go down?" Oh, I just pulled my necklace off and showed him. I thought, he's a cutie. He's a big flirt.

The band that was playing recognized Hector, and they announced his name. We started dancing, and I tripped us because of my feet and we fell. Oh my gosh, it was fun, and I was just laughing the whole time. I was thrilled.

Hector: That's when I asked you if you would go out with me and you said yes. I was a skinny little man. I was a skinny man because I only weighed like 120 pounds because I just got over my accident. I wasn't eating that much because I couldn't. I had to eat soups and stuff like that. I took her out to dinner several times, but I was embarrassed because I couldn't eat that well. But she didn't care, she said fine.

Carol: That didn't bother me at all. Once we were going out, I could see he still had some pain. I'm a natural therapeutic specialist and I work with people, hands on. And just to see him, I wanted to put my hands on him and work with him. And I could see things in him, like with his neck and his head. And so I couldn't wait to work on him. I still do if he needs it. I'll work on his lower back and his neck and shoulders, or whatever it might be.

Hector: But, on top of all that, I went through a lot of depression. She went through it with me. I was depressed because I was not playing guitar. I was just very depressed because I think the medication made me that way. I tried to commit suicide a couple of times and she knew that. And my brothers knew that too. So they stopped me from committing suicide. I didn't know what I was thinking. I had a gun, and I pointed to my head, because I didn't want to live anymore at that point, because I was helpless. But when she came along, a lot of the depression went away because she lifted me up. She lifted my spirits up. So that's where she came in. It was some crazy times in my life. I'm glad I didn't commit suicide.

In 2008, I started playing at the Santa Ana Casino for the first time. I was playing for the Sunday Brunches. That's the first gig that I got after the accident. I was playing there and a good friend of mine was a manager there, Leo Bryant. He was a manager, and we worked together for a long time, but he knew that I was coming out of my accident, so he gave me work. That was very kind of him to do that.

But I was struggling, but I did it, though I was still struggling through my music. And people understood that. There's some people that were a little sad to see me struggling like that because they never saw me like that.

Carol would come with me and shortly after, we played together at Santa Ana. She helped me and performed with me.

After that, I met this beautiful lady at the casino, Rita Benavidez, of Casa de Benavidez, and they were sitting at a table in the casino. I remember playing for her when I was 21 years old at the restaurant. I sat down next to her and she recognized me. She said, "Hector, how are you?"

"I'm doing good. I'm doing better since the accident."

"Do you wanna come play in my restaurant?"

I said, "Yeah, yeah. I would love to."

So I got more work. I was still struggling, but she gave me the work. I got better because I was performing more and more because that's what I wanted to do. She hired me and I've been playing for them since, I guess, at the end of 2008, for 16 years.

I also got hired to do private parties and events again. In 2007, the Minor League All-Star Baseball Game was held at the Rio Grande Credit Union Isotopes Park, here in Albuquerque. That was a big event, and I got to play that. In April 2013, I played at the inaugural opening of JetBlue airlines at the Albuquerque Sunport.

Somewhere around 2010, I played for a meeting of executives for Presbyterian Hospital that was in Washington, D.C. at the Hay-Adams Hotel, right across from the White House.

Over the last 10 or 15 years, I've played for oil companies in Hobbs, New Mexico. We also played for a Little League Fundraiser in Farmington,

I told Carol one time when we first got married, I will be making coffee for you in the mornings because what the Bible says. The man has always has to make coffee for the wife in the morning, so ever since then I've been making coffee every morning for her.

"Yeah, he makes coffee. He's so sweet."

And that's what I told her. That's what the Bible says.

New Mexico. They liked us so much that a restaurant owner asked us to stay for another week and play at his restaurant. So we did.

I also got to play at a reception for balloonists Troy Bradley and Leonid Tiukhtyaev, who broke the distance record for a gas balloon in 2015. It was a big deal here in Alburquerque because the command center was here when they did the flight. It was a fun reception and it was wonderful to meet them both.

I was trying to recover and the more I played, the better I got. The more I studied with Mr.

Garcia, the better I got. And then I started to get better and better and better from getting back into my music. And then, of course, my family, my brothers, and my mom and dad were there for me all the time. I've got a good family. They were awesome. And my family was there for me. They helped me a lot spiritually. They help me to do what I was born to do.

Hector, left, and Carol, right, with record breaking balloonists Troy Bradley and Russian Leonid Tiukhtyaev.

Bryan's
PHOTOGRAPHY

Love and Music

I play, for example, classical music, like Spanish classical. I'm learning a song and it is one of the prettiest classical pieces that I have ever heard in my life. It's called "The Marriage of Love." I love romantic music. I love that it's going to have a lot of drama in it. I mean, without drama in music, there's no music at all. I mean, you've got to have that in there, that passion in my music. If you don't have that, if a musician doesn't have that, he cannot prove it to the audience. He's not a musician. He's just a person playing with a metronome. I tell my students you need emotion. You're listening to a conversation. That's what I love about it.

You get involved with it. You're getting involved with a person's emotions, too. While you're listening to me, you're getting involved with me, too. It's like making love to a person with a passion.

When I'm playing at a restaurant, a lot of times it's hard to put the passion that you want to. Because there's so many people and people listening, but you still do. You still wanna do your best, but you have to try to do your best for everybody. Sometimes I ask, how do you think I did? They'd say, "You did wonderful." But to me, it's like, I didn't do it the way I wanted to because. you're focused on music. But when you're still playing, you know, the music is your effort into playing the best you can, and making people happy, and enjoying the music I play.

I started recording and came out with several CDs. One of my first compositions was for my daughter, Infania, and I recorded that. In fact, it was the first song in the album. The next was Feugo, another composition of mine.

There are different techniques for different music. For example, flamenco. But the music that I really enjoy playing is a softer., the more romantic music .This other stuff is good. I mean, it's exciting, but it's not what I like to play. My favorite is romantic music. It's a passion that I have about that kind of style of music.

I like listening to all kinds of music, but lately I've been listening to French classical guitarist Emmanuel Rossfelder. Also, Ana Vidović, of course, and Spanish guitarist and composer Paco de Lucía, who plays nuevo flamenco.

Going back to my recovery from my accident, it was a long road. It was only because I had been playing since I was a boy. Your brain is going to heal, and it does heal, especially with music. You know music is a very strong element for the brain and the brain can be healed by itself, eventually. Music can be powerful for people that are sick and people that have traumas. Music is great therapy.

Because I'm a musician, I've had the chance to meet and get to know many wonderful people. I'm very blessed because that's what music does. You bring people together with music. Because of everything that I've done and the people I've performed for. I've met so many beautiful, great people. They're gracious. They're loving people to me and I love them all.

Hector Pimentel by Dallas

Funny story. I had this guitar that my brother has just finished making for me. I had several guitars, and when I die, my kids are going to take the guitars. Well, a guitar that I gave to my youngest daughter Rachel had the Phantom of the opera on the face. I got it back from my daughter and I forgot that I had given it to her. That was years ago.

So, one day Rachel asks, "Dad, do you think I can have my guitar back?"

I said, "Oh, no." You know what I told her? "I forgot that I gave you the guitar. But I got a new one."

"No, I want the phantom of the opera guitar."

"Honey, my brother just sold that to somebody in California."

"Why'd you do that?"

She got mad at me, and she wouldn't talk to me. The guitar was gone.

About 5-6 months later, the guitar came back from California. I saw the guitar here in the shop. I asked what's going on with the guitar? Were they going to repair it? What happened to it? I was told the guy traded it in for another guitar. I told my brother, "Let me give you my guitar you just made for me and I'll take that one back."

My brother asked "Why?"

"Because I gave that to my daughter, and she keeps asking for it. And she's gonna be surprised once she gets it back."

My brother said, "Are you sure? Because the new one's more expensive than that one."

I said, "Yeah, but you know, my daughter's mad at me right now. I gotta give that guitar back." So my brother said, "OK, you can have back."

So I called my daughter. "Guess what? I got guitar back!"

"Really?"

"Yeah." So she got all happy about that. I guess it was meant to be.

Rick Pimentel

Brother, President and Master Guitar Builder

As far as a musician, I think he's one of the best as far as classical guitar players that has brought music to New Mexico in such a way that most people haven't. And he's brought electronics into a classical guitar, which he's one of the first that started that idea, which I think is great. A lot of people at that time when he first started playing the guitar, didn't even think about it, trying to put it in a classical guitar. Acoustic guitar, great, but classical guitar, they weren't. So that's one good thing about my brother, that he developed that idea, you know, here in New Mexico and a lot of people followed that.

He's a good teacher and a good musician. But as far as my brother's concerned, I would never take lessons from him because he's family.

I'm not a guitar player, I'm a master builder and that's what I love doing. The music to me is secondary. But, as far as he's concerned, you know, that was his passion. He was also pushed into it by my father. He put that in place music into his soul because at one time there was a place where he fought it. And my father just pushed it, pushed it, and made that dream come true in his own mind.

And so my father had a lot to do with Hector becoming a good musician. Because Hector fought him as well. But I think my father did the same thing with us as far as guitar makers. I mean, there was a point where we fought him to do what he did, you know? But I actually fell in love with this, with my father's passion, when we were kids. So that's why I followed that dream, you know. But still we had a lot of fights during that time. Because, in the business, it was slow and you're not making the money you want to make. Monetarily, you're poor, and you're young and you want to create a family and you know you want to excel and do something different. But we could see the dream and so we're stuck with it. It was the same with Hector. As far as music is concerned, he saw that dream, and so he took it to a place where most musicians here in New Mexico haven't done, which is a really great thing for him and a lot of people do follow him. A lot of people are jealous of him, you know, and so they talk badly about his ideas and what he's done because they're jealous. And I don't blame them because he put himself on the map here in New Mexico by doing the music that he loves and teaching the people. He's very friendly with most people. People love him as far as a person and that is reflected in his music and performances, which is really a good thing. So I think his music is some of the best. He follows a lot of ideas from some of the great musicians out there, like Chet Atkins. He loves that type of music. And so he kind of followed that idea. But he listens to a lot of musicians all over and gets ideas, then puts it into his own, which is a good thing in a musician. So I think he's done great things with his music. So, as I said before, people love him and they follow his music, and they respect him, which is a good thing, too. And even the great musicians that are playing today. Like Ben Perea, five time banjo champion. He did take lessons with Hector, and he learned a lot from Hector. His teaching helps everybody and their style of music. And then they take it to a different place. And so Hector has a lot to do with that, with a lot of musicians. And most musicians here in New Mexico that have made it, he had some role in it, which is really a good thing. So as far as a musician, I think he's one of the best, you know, and I love him for it.

Family is always the best you can have in a place of any kind of business. It takes you that much further when you respect each other. We are guitar makers. It's our brand. So we really push it hard and we're out there all over the world, pushing our guitars and talking to people. Our business is sort of word of mouth. People respect our company and our guitars. Hector wouldn't be who he is without our company, and that's a fact. My father's legacy is something unique in today's world of guitars because he kept the idea of handmade products. Today, it's almost nil in the world of guitars. Everything is so mass produced. So we kept that legacy going and made it better and still are continuing that legacy of making it, creating it and making it that much better. So that helps Hector as well because the name Pimentel is very strong in guitars. Not necessarily music, but in guitars. But that helps him as a guitarist and that helps us as guitar makers. So it really mixes really very, very well, you know, but it's not one that makes the company, it's when you're together that makes that strong, and makes the family strong and the business strong as far as music and guitar making. It's a great thing. It's not just Hector. It's all of it. That's what makes the name. Music, guitars, it all blends together very well. There's nothing better in the world.

For the family, my mother is a great backbone. She was my father's backbone, and she was our backbone. Without her, I don't think we would have what we have because she was strong in what she wanted us to do and she's the one that really pushed my dad to be who he wanted to be. Because without her, he wouldn't have gotten this far. I'll tell you that for a fact. She was very strong, and she loved the fact that my dad had his business with guitars. She loves guitars. She loves music. So she's the one that pushed him, even though she knew she was going to starve. She pushed him. She said, "We'll make it," even with 12 kids, and that was the point where we starved. But she was still right there. We're going to make it. She was a strong backbone. I love my mother and I take care of her. I go to her house every day and so make sure she's well. Whatever she needs in this world, I take care of it. We can't do without our mothers. She was a true backbone for music, for guitars, for everything, so we have to thank her for where we are today. We respect her a lot.

Hector has done a lot in music for the state. We respect that a lot and he's done very well for our guitars as well. He uses them. He loves them. He talks great about them, which is really a good thing. And we respect the idea that he plays our guitars because without him, we probably would miss that, so I'm glad that this is together.

It's so true with every musician that's playing Pimentel guitars from all over the world, all over the United States. People ask where did you get that guitar? It's a Pimentel! Not only does that help us, it helps him create a bigger name. Hector gets up there and starts talking about the guitars and pushing the guitars and says this guitar was made by my brother and he's got so much passion and he loves it. I do respect that and I hear other people tell me what he says about the guitars. So it gets my heart. I love that.

There are so many musicians out there that play our guitars, for instance, Mel Bay Publications out of St. Louis, Missouri. They're one of the biggest publications in the world as far as music publications go. They always have Pimentel guitars on the covers of the classical guitar music books. These are all Pimentel guitars. One of the books that has a Pimentel on it was way back when they first started using Pimentel guitars and they put it on the cover and it's been on the cover for thirty or forty years, which is really a good thing. So Mel Bay plays one of my acoustic guitars and that's what he teaches with, but also has a 12 string guitar my brother made. My father used to work with Mel Bay because Mel Bay loved my dad. So yeah, so there's there's a lot that's happened to within our company. Our guitar is the state guitar of New Mexico.

So there's so much about Pimentel Guitars that has been great for our company, and Hector is a big part, for sure. Without Hector, it would be hard. It's a very good balance. I appreciate him, but as I said, he's a good musician. He's done so much in music that a lot of people learned from him. We make fun of him once in a while, but we love that. He's a good musician, a good brother. He's a good man.

Robert Pimentel

Brother, Vice President and Master Guitar Builder

Of course, I've known Hector for all my life because he's my brother. I am his manager, and I manage some of his gigs. There' are a lot of gigs that we get for his music and every time we do a gig, then, of course, I charge according to what he's going to play and who he's going to play for. A lot of times we play for Presbyterian hospitals, or parties that are associated with the Balloon Festival, or just big organizations that are that are looking for a musician like Hector that wants to play guitar and play well. He's a very good guitarist, that's for sure. He's one of the best guitarists that I've heard. Even though he's my brother. I'm not trying to be , but he is very good on the guitar. I make his guitars and I'm also his manager, so I manage his music. Anytime that there is something that's coming up, I ask him if he's got the time to do it and he'll say yes because I know he plays in restaurants as well. A lot of times people want to use him for restaurants, but because he's so committed to Casa de Benavidez, we cannot use them for other gigs on those days. But there's other times we can use him for Saturdays, Sundays, or private parties and things

like that. So that's where I come in, and do the contracts.

I manage other musicians as well, but whenever somebody calls for music, I recommend Hector. First of all, he plays my guitars which is important to me, that he plays Pimentel Guitars. The other thing is that the quality of music that he performs is wonderful. I get the feedback that, oh man, this was a wonderful gig. Can we use him again? I say, of course, anytime you're ready for another gig, just let me know and we'll set him up again.

He's not inexpensive. He's high dollar according to other musicians. But people prefer him because he's well known for his music. All this came out from my father's legacy. For us as well as Hector. If it wasn't for my father, then he wouldn't be where he's at. Oh. He played trombone or one of those brass instruments when he was young. So Hector used to ask my dad, "Where's my trombone?" My dad would say, "You don't have no goddamn trombone. You're going to play the guitar." So that's how he got more into the guitar as a kid and he started learning how to perform with it as an instrument in his younger age. When he was 18 or

20 years old, he started playing at restaurants.

Hector had very good instructors at that time, because there were a lot of musicians here. We still have a lot of musicians here, but they're not quite the same. But at one time in the 70s and 80s, we had a lot of musicians here. We had Alberto Marin, Vicente Saucedo, and groups that play Pimentel guitars. And Hector was right along with them, playing in restaurants and things like that. He was also doing a lot of gigs and since then he's been doing real well as far as music's concerned and I'm happy to help him out whenever I can. I rather use him than anybody else unless they want to group. Hector had a group before and we were using them for the Hilton hotel and other gigs that we would get. And then we even did a concert here in New Mexico. I forgot what city it was or what town it was, but they paid quite a bit of money to send the whole group up there. We sent back a thank you note because they paid really well. And the group was very, very nice. We were playing at the Hilton and other events.

So basically, Hector is doing well with the instrument and I think he's going to continue doing that till he dies. Like we're going to continue working here till we die here.

When I was younger, I learned music from my father. My father didn't read music. He just listened to the song. He played it and he was a pretty good guitarist. I wanted to learn with him and so I would sit with him and play the guitar. He'd say, "Just listen to me. If you know the song, you should be able to play it." And that's how I started learning a lot of songs. But then, after my father passed away, I went to Hector and asked him, "Can you do this for me?" Like, just write it the way I write it because I have a special way of writing my music. And he said, so I'll figure it out. I'll write it in a certain way so that you can understand it. And so he has been writing some music, but I don't go up there and listen or take a lesson with him. I just go through the music. If I know the song, I should be able to play it. So that's how I learned. But Hector is a good teacher as well because he has a lot of patience with his students. Some students don't want to learn classical guitar because classical guitar is complicated. And a lot of people don't want to learn the hard way. A lot of them do, but a lot of them don't. A lot of them just want to play a song that they can enjoy and go home and play a little, like *Love Me Tender* or something or *Vaya Con Dios*. Just something simple. And so there are a lot of students that have taken lessons with different instructors here who have actually quit and some of them are coming back to go to Hector because Hector is easy. He teaches whatever they want to learn. Whether it's an easy song, it doesn't have to be complicated with classical music. Once they learn the easy stuff, then they can go harder and harder. But some don't want to start reading music and don't want him saying "OK. Here's the book. Learn this." And I don't want to either. I mean, I don't want to take another year to learn how to read notes when I can already play a little bit here and there and if I know the song. I just have to practice it and do it my way, or no way at all.

So I think that's the best way to approach the public as far as them wanting to learn music and not try to make them learn the hard stuff that they'll never learn. They're never going to become a guitarist that's going to do a concert with classical guitar. Some of them will, but they're going to a higher class. They're going to universities and are studying with Pepe Romero or somebody with a big name. And those are the ones that are going for the classical. But the ones here, the older people, they just want to learn something simple and it's hard for some to teach that. So we send them to Hector and he'll teach them whatever they want. And they're pretty much happy all the time. They keep coming back. So, as far as teaching is concerned, I think it's great. I think he plays really well and I'll continue using him as long as I keep getting calls for his music.

We get calls for him maybe 3 or 4 times a month for different organizations, weddings, parties, private parties. There's a retirement home, I can't remember the name, but they'll email me and they'll ask if Hector has time to play on this date, which is a Tuesday or something like that. And then they'll tell me, well, we can only pay $150.00 for two hours. I tell them that's not going to happen. You know, you either pay my price or don't do it at all, or find somebody else. Then they say, for Hector, we'll pay the price. I booked several other people, not just Hector, but I do book other people as well, but depends on what they want, like the Mariachi group, or they want something different like a trio. So I'm doing different musicians, but mostly I use Hector.

I try to keep his bookings to museums, private organizations that are more artistic. Ones that have art. They want classical music or popular music or something the guitarists can enjoy while they're eating or snacking or just looking at the art. And he does play classical music. So if somebody wants classical pieces, then he can do it. I remember one time when he was younger, a radio station asked him to play Mexican music. He said, "Oh no, I don't play that shit." And now he plays it all the time! So you know when you're young, you're trying to do something different and you don't understand the concept of all music. But he does now. He plays anything and everything, whether it's country and western, or whether it's Mexican music. And he's always learning new stuff, all the time. He'll say, "Hey, Robert, look at this. I just learned this new song." Wow, that's cool.It's going to be nice when you play it at the restaurant, or wherever you want to play it.

My role here is vice president. I used to make steel string guitars with Rick a long time ago, when we were doing the competitions in Kansas and in Kirby, Texas. And I made classical guitars, too. I was making guitars a level down from my father, so I was making Roswell guitars and concert instruments, but not premier guitars like my father was making. So when my father passed away, I took over his line. So now I do all the high end classical guitars. I do jazz fusions, 7 strings, 8 strings, 10 strings, 12 strings, classicals, jazz, fusion, tekintos, flamencos. So I have a variety of instruments that I make, but they're all at the higher end.So Hector's guitar is a jazz fusion. IT has electronics in it because a lot of people like electronics. They like Hector, for example, he's got to have electronics to play because, otherwise, he's playing for a big group. A lot of people like those because it's a Fishman system that you just plug in and you're ready to go. It's simple.

Hector likes the jazz fusions, so he wants me to make him another one. I'm still debating on that one. I'll probably wind up making another guitar sometime soon. Just right now I'm booked with other instruments that I'm making, but he does deserve another guitar.

When I make guitars, I start with seven or eight guitars. Every time I start a batch, I finish those in about a month and a half to two months. It depends on what it is and how much inlay is with it. Right now I have a few of them that are waiting to be picked up and they're very expensive guitars, like $45,000 and there's another one for $20,000. I'm putting their names on it and they chose the rosewood and they're happy to pay $15,000 or $20,000. That's what I do. I do the grand concert high end guitars.In fact, Mel Bay ordered a 12 string classical guitar. I made it, but the company that we order gears from, nobody had 12 string gears for 12 string classical guitars. They make steel strings gears in 12 strings, but never in a classical. The company Alessi Tuning Machines in Italy decided to make the gears for us and now they are selling them online for 12 strings classical guitars. They decided to get that line in their service, which is cool. This business is amazing to me because we're a family of guitar makers and musicians, and people are happier with our guitars then they are with Martins or Taylors or anything else.

Victor Pimentel

Brother and Master Guitar Builder

Hector is a good guitarist, and he's a really good teacher. He does a great job with the students and does teaching in the manner where they like the way he teaches. He's a great teacher and a great guitar player. I think his wife plays too sometimes with him. She plays the congas or something like that. I've seen them both play together. They do a good job together, too. Sometimes I go to see him play at Casa de Benavidez. They had great food there and when he plays there and everybody seems to have a wonderful time when he's playing. He's a funny guy and makes everybody laugh. He's a hit.

Like I said, he is a great teacher. I've heard that little kids like him and old people get along with him. You might go to another teacher that he's teaching you like, you know, I gotta read the notes; you gotta do. I gotta do like that. And you say, I can't learn like that. I don't wanna be a professional. I just wanna play for myself. Hector is the kind of person that can teach that way. To have somebody play a couple songs and they're happy with that, then later on they'll play more songs. So he's actually a really good teacher, and

he's actually a really good guitar player. When you're teaching a person one on one, you learn more if you got a good teacher. You learn a lot more. And he's teaching the way the person wants to learn. Some people can listen to music and play. Some people can read the music and learn how to play that way. He teaches all that.

I play a bit, but I can't learn from my brother. So Juanito teaches me. I play some music and then Hector will ask, what song are you playing? He goes, "Oh, I know that song. There's a better way to play it." And I say, "Hector, I'm not interested." And then a month later, after I got to learn how to play the song better , I was playing right here and he was upstairs and he says, "That was good! You did good on that song." And I said, "Yeah, thank you." But it's just hard to learn from my brother. Brotherly love, right?

I started learning from my dad at one time and he would teach me a few songs or a few chords and stuff like that. I would like to learn but I was always busy, and other than working here. I didn't have time to play, but when I'd go home and he would ask me to play a little bit and I learned a little bit that way, but I've always wanted to learn more songs because when we were kids, we got to learn how to play notes and stuff like that and what the tone should be on the guitar, like that to learn the guitar making part of it.

But you know, I've always wanted to learn a little bit more. So, Hector Garcia was playing teaching here at one time, so I learned from him, too. He was teaching Robert at the same time, and Robert was learning a different way from what I was learning. And Hector Garcia would get mixed up and he would teach me Robert's way. I'd say, "You're teaching me two different ways. I can't learn like that." Then he would forget because he was already old.

When I was growing up, my dad always wanted me next to him to learn his way of building guitars. So that's the way I started off and I've always made classical guitars. And then later on in the years, my dad actually made a lute. I was going to school for architecture so I took drafting , advanced drafting, engineering, geometry and mathematics. So one day I came to the shop and one day my dad was building this lute and was trying to put the whole back together to make it look like a dome. My dad was having some problems while he was trying to make the mold. So I came home and I ask, "What are you trying to do, Dad?" He says, "I'm trying to make this flat but the angle is wrong." I asked, "What angle are you using?" And he says he had it

on 30° on the table to sand to make it flat. And I said, "Well, that's your problem. If you angle between the banana strips is 30 degrees, you need 15 degrees on the edge to make that flat." He didn't believe me at first, but I started doing it for him and then he saw. "You're right." So he finished it off and then I helped him bend the sides for the lute and helped him put it together. So I did help him with it and that was his first lute that he made. Then he made a potbelly mandolin. So he did different instruments. He was the only one that would build exotic and specialty instruments. So I guess I took that place. Now I make classical guitars, steel strings, flamencos, then the ukulele started coming out. People wanted ukuleles, so Rick said you can do that and I said yeah. So I started making ukuleles. And then, all of a sudden, they wanted mandolins. And so Rick told me you need to make the mandolins and we'll design it together and you make it. So I started doing that. It's a lot harder than guitar or ukulele because of the curve on the mandolin and the back of it as well. So it's a lot more difficult and they're smaller. So you're going to put your hands in there and then when it comes to electronics, you have to do it before while it's still open and put electronics inside. So I master in ukuleles and mandolins and guitars. So I do it all.

This is the most important thing. While I was growing up and my dad was making me build guitars, he says, "In order for you to become the best guitar maker in the world, if you can get a guitar that's completely broken and fix it, make it look like there was never ever broken, that's how you'll know. Then you'll be one of the best guitar makers in the world." So I've done that. We've gotten guitars that are broken and this and that cracked in here, lifted up different ways and I'm able to fix it and make it look like brand new again. The people that got their guitar back could say, "I can't believe this is my guitar!" So that makes you really good at what you do. That's what my dad instilled in me.

Pimentel & Sons Guitar Makers

The Pimentel Sons, Rick, Robert and Victor, all master guitar makers, will make the guitar, mandolin, or ukulele of your dreams. All built with exquisite craftsmanship by hand with the finest materials.

The New Mexico Sunrise Guitar, the Official State Guitar of New Mexico.

Congressional Record

PROCEEDINGS AND DEBATES OF THE 115th CONGRESS, FIRST SESSION

United States of America

Vol. 163	WASHINGTON, WEDNESDAY, FEBRUARY 15, 2017	*No. 27*

Senate & House Representatives
RECOGNIZING PIMENTEL & SONS GUITARMAKERS

Mr. HEINRICH. Mr. President, it is an honor to join musicians and music lovers in recognizing Albuquerque's Pimentel family for their 65 years of building handcrafted instruments that are sought after by guitar players and collectors around the world.

Pimentel & Sons is a successful family-owned small business that was started from scratch and has been sustained with innovation, hard work, and a commitment to excellence.

As the ranking member on the Joint Economic Committee, I am proud to recognize successful entrepreneurs and small business owners like the Pimentels.

Lorenzo Pimentel learned the craft of building guitars as a teenager in Ciudad Juarez. After marrying his wife, Josefina, Lorenzo moved his family to Albuquerque after falling in love with the Sandia Mountains. Over his lifetime, Lorenzo Pimentel accumulated an incredible list of accolades for his guitars.

Four of Lorenzo's sons, Agustin, Ricardo, Roberto, and Victor, have continued their late father's work as master guitar makers in their own right. They have each played an integral role in shaping New Mexico's music scene for decades.

Pimentel & Sons has earned the Hispanic Heritage Month Distinguished Honor Award, the Governor's Award for Excellence and Achievement in the Arts, and an invitation to the Smithsonian Institute's Festival of American Folklife.

In 2009, Governor Bill Richardson signed a bill designating Pimentel's Sunrise model as the official State guitar of New Mexico.

Generations of musicians have played and appreciated the world-renowned Pimentel guitars that capture the spirit and culture of New Mexico.

Ms. Lujan Grisham: Mr. Speaker: I rise today to acknowledge the 65th Anniversary of Pimentel & Sons Guitar Makers, a company that has become synonymous with traditional, handcrafted musical instruments.

Sincerely,

Michelle Lujan Grisham

MICHELLE LUJAN GRISHAM
Member of Congress

Infania Pimentel

Hector's Daughter

I'll start from the accident because that was obviously a big moment in my life. I was really young. I remember I was with my family and we were having dinner and he was giving a performance at Pope Joy Hall, I believe. Me and my mom and my siblings were at the kitchen, and I remember my mom got a phone call and she picked up the call. She didn't really say anything. She just got very serious and said everyone, we need to get in the car and so we got in the car.

Whenever we got to the library, I remember it was night time and it was very dark. My siblings were freaking out. They were crying really hard. But something that always, in that moment, stuck with me was my mom would always tell me, in really big life moments you have to keep composure. She had gotten out of the car to go see what was going on with my dad. I didn't see my dad, but I saw a huge puddle of blood and my siblings were freaking out and crying. And as the 8 year old there, I remember thinking, "Oh my God, I'm the only adult here. I have to calm my siblings. I was the oldest, so I'm trying to calm my siblings down.

Not knowing exactly what was the situation with my dad, I was just hoping for the best. Time went by and he was in ICU. I remember the first time I was able to see him. It was me and my mom and we went through different curtains of patients and I saw a bunch of different people in different types of conditions and I saw this man and he looked really bad. His face was really puffy and different colors and I thought he looked almost like a clown. Really, really badly beaten up and I just smiled at him. But I was kind of scared. I kept walking to the next curtain. My mom told me, say hi to your dad and yeah, that person that I didn't recognize was my dad. That was obviously like really shocking, but I remember that I really wanted to take care of him.

After that he was in all the different stages. When he got to go home he was in a wheelchair. I wanted to push him around even when he was moving on to the walker. I would say no, stay in the wheelchair. I wanted to push you. Obviously he just kept getting better. He went from the walker to the cane.

What I do remember is my dad's personality

before the accident. My dad has always been super amazing, but with music he was very strict. He he loved classical music and flamenco and those traditional styles of music. But he was a lot more lenient after that. I guess because he's had a brain injury, so I guess whenever different parts of the brain are injured, it could affect personality and things like that. So at least with music choice, that was something that stuck with me. Now he's fine with any type of music and he loves it all, so that's really cool.

Growing up, he's always been kind of a fighter and in the way that he's always wanted what's best for his kids. And he would fight to the end of the world to make sure that that was the case. We were in good situations. As for the type of father he is, he's always been. Above and beyond amazing.

He was very protective as a dad and still is. I think now as an adult I have really high standards when it comes to partners because I've seen my dad. I don't know if he ever really told me no, but he never really stuck to a no with me. I feel like he does everything with the kindness of his heart. He was a very romantic partner to my mom and now to his current wife. It has been really special to see. I think my brother's got a lot of those traits from him, too.

Growing up and seeing him play music has been super amazing. Seeing him play with different bands, it was always super cool and inspiring. It made me want to play guitar, too.

He tried teaching me when I was young. Probably before his accident, I want to say honestly when I was like 7 years old, so maybe around the time that he had the accident and I wasn't interested at the time. That's funny. I think it probably did happen before the accident because he wanted me to learn how to play guitar or how to read music and was very strict about that. I wasn't interested in learning how to read music. But I always loved hearing him play like I could watch him play and hear him play all day. I never got bored. And after his accident, probably when I was 11 or 12 years old is when I picked it up. I picked it up on the condition that he would not require me to learn how to read music. And so there's another personality trait. So he taught me how to play now. He'll teach me a song and he'll tell me where to put my fingers. Now, I'm 27 years old and so ask, "Dad, where to put my fingers? I don't know how to read music."

I actually went to music school briefly in high school in Santa Fe. It was for guitar. I was the only woman who got accepted to the program and also the only one who didn't know how to read music. I went for there for a very short period of time because I would have to commute every day and it was a lot for me. I graduated from La Cueva High School, then I went to college at UNM and now I'm in graduate school at Tufts in Boston. I'm learning about surgical robotics for brain surgery. After my dad's injury, I really wanted to help in that field

So the place I ended up graduating and getting my undergrad from UNM, we were in the back of the library where my dad's accident happened. And I know that now because I spent so much time there and I am able to recollect the two moments.

Since this semester started in particular, has been very difficult. So I have not had the time to practice. I'm pretty sure I've only taken out my guitar once since summer started. It's really hard to practice nowadays with school. I'm very fortunate to have a guitar that my grandfather built when I was born. It is named after me.

Something else about my dad. When I lived with him in high school, because at one point I moved in to live with him full time, I remember every morning he would make me breakfast. My dad didn't cook much, but he always made breakfast for me, and he would make me hot cocoa every morning. And I remember doughnuts on Sunday is something that he would always do. I always thought that was really cute.

He's very special to me. I think guitars helped us have a very special type of relationship.

Hector with Infania at her High School graduation.

Infania Pimentel

Doctoral Student in Mechanical Engineering

Rachael Pimentel

Hector's Daughter

Growing up with him, I felt like I was his little princess. So was my sister. He was a good dad. He did a lot for us. And he fought for us really hard with my mom. I feel like he's definitely a man that I look up to. There was like a lot of back and forth with my mom and my dad and he kept fighting for his kids. Which I feel like is a good thing because, like a lot of men out there, they don't do that. I feel like he will do anything for us. There's never been a dull moment with him. I mean, sure, we've had arguments, because we were teenagers, but we don't appreciate things our parents do.

I've seen him perform pretty much all my life. I've seen him at restaurants, but I've also seen him doing concerts. I tried to pick up guitar, but I could never get the hang of it. My sister, Infania, plays, though.

I had a Pimentel guitar. One time I asked him, "Where's my guitar?"

And he says, "Honey, I broke it."

I was like, "I hope you're gonna get it fixed."

"No, honey, it's not fixable. I'm sorry."

I was so hurt. My heart was shattered. Then he told me a couple of years later, after he had told me it broke and it shattered, like I was never going to get my guitar back, he said "Honey, I have to tell you something."

"What?"

He said, "But you can't get mad at me."

I'm like, "What?"

And he says "I sold your guitar."

"What? Excuse me?"

"Yeah, honey, I sold your guitar, but I got it back."

"Okay."

"But you can't get mad because they had it painted a different color."

I was so upset because I loved the color that it was originally because it was like a maroonish color. And now it's like a tan color. And I don't really like it. So I told him, "Well, I hope that you get it back to the color that it used to be."

It's still a tan color, but he said he was gonna get it painted, but I don't know.

Yeah, he told me it was broken. Then a few years later, he comes and tells me he sold it, but he got it back. So it's okay.

I did see him play a lot when I was younger,

because we were around more. But I've seen him play at UNM. He traveled a lot though, too. I know that they went to Japan. I want to say Mexico, but I'm not too sure. I don't even think I was born yet when all that happened. I know that he did play for one of the presidents. Not too sure which one, though.

When I was younger, my dad would sneak into my room and he'd say, come on, let's go. And he'd say, don't wake up your brother and sister. We're gonna go to Dunkin' Donuts. And so he would take me to Dunkin' Donuts. And I was his coffee buddy. So he would wake me up like almost every morning to go to Dunkin' Donuts. He'd be like, don't wake up your brother and sister. He'd say, let's just go, so we would just do that together, which was really nice.

I feel like me and my dad whenever I was younger, we were really close. We were like best friends. Even in high school, too, before he would take me to school every morning, he would take me to Starbucks or McDonald's. It was like an every morning thing. And I would tell him, I think it was more in the high school era, I don't have a first period in the morning. Can we like go get something? I would be very late and a couple of times my dad did get in trouble for that too.

Another time, whenever I was barely starting to drive, I think I was like 16 or 17. I had only had my permit, and I convinced my dad somehow to let me get a car. I told him I have my license and then he was like, oh, really? He's said, let me see it. I kind of showed it to him fast. And yeah, he didn't realize that it was only my permit. I don't think I have told him that yet, either. So I ended up with the car, anyway.

My dad is a really good dad. Growing up, he was always there. He was always there, with school, with things with my mom. Like whenever he would fight with my mom and stuff like that, he was always there. He has been a really good dad.

At one point, I was living with him alone. I think my brother was living at my moms at the time and my sister might have been living with her boyfriend at the time. And so it was just me at the house. My dad always let me have my friends over and he always let me go hang out with my friends and do things like that.

I have a son, 4 years old, and he actually goes to the school where I work. He started going there a little bit before I started working there. I needed a job at the time and I was like, what better place to work? So I ended up working there. And I love it. The kids are cool.

I feel like the whole family is kind of separated right now. My brother's in Austin. My sister's in Boston. I'm here.

Robert Pimentel II

Hector's nephew and Student

As a young kid, obviously music is in my blood, right? I'm born and raised with music. I'd always come into the shop as a kid and see my dad and uncles building these guitars and wondering, oh, wow, this is cool. And then by the time when I grew up, it was pretty popular to play like rock'n'roll music. Metallica was one of my favorite bands. So I was like, oh man, I want to aspire to learn Metallica music and just try to play the electric guitar. So I was talking to my uncle Hector one day and, of course, him being in the music industry and playing for so long, I said, "Hey, do you think you could teach me a Metallica song?"

He starts laughing. He's like, "What do you want to learn?"

"Metallica, because it's my favorite band, you know?" And it was. It's just something that I wanted to do and I wanted to be a rock star, and I wanted to play electric guitar and all this.

He said, "You know, I'll tell you what, if you were to learn classical music or flamenco music, you'll be able to learn anything." And so it kind of resonated with me. I'm like, OK, I don't really like that kind of music. But you're telling me if I learn

it, then I can learn anything. So bells started going off in my head. And I'm like, oh, well, I still want to learn how to play Metallica. So, OK, I'll give it a shot.

He said, "Why don't you come to my studio and I'll just start teaching you."

I said, "OK, cool, of course."

He's always done it for free for me because I'm his nephew and what not. So he was teaching me the basics. He showed me how to play certain notes and chords and then he started writing what's called tablature. He started writing tablature for me because I didn't really know the theory of how to read music. You have to really study it and learn. So his way of teaching really resonated with me just because when he taught me something, I actually learned how to play a song. I didn't have to worry about learning how to read the music and why it was written the way it was written, the theory behind it. So it really resonated with me because after taking a couple of lessons with him, I could actually play a full song. And I think to the average person that doesn't really care too much about the theory of the music, they just want to know how to play a song. I'm not going to speak for everybody, but for me, at the time I was like, just teach me. I could just learn, and I kind of already had an ear for music. Don't ask me why, but I would pick up the guitar and I would learn stuff on my own as well. So I'd listen to the song Metallica in particular, and then I'd, yeah, I'd just pick it up. I figured it out, and I started playing, just learning by listening. When Hector got to me, he started teaching me a mixture of classical, but then I wanted him to teach me flamenco, because I felt like flamenco was more my style, so to speak. And then just the complexity of how you play flamenco. I mean, there are certain techniques and I remember picking up the guitar and taking my first lesson with Hector. I'd have the guitar in a way that I had it balanced on my right leg and he told me you've got to position the whole body of the guitar between your legs. I never really knew that. I was sloppily playing the guitar, and he goes, no position it this way and then your hands, you have to position them in a certain way. I never knew that. He started teaching me the basics. And then it got to the point where I actually learned how to play a whole song. I'm like, this is cool. I can do this.

So that's how my relationship with Hector grew from that point. I've always been around my family. It's just the nature of the beast. But it just kind of grew from that point. And then I was

enamored by him. This guy can play really well. And then it struck me. Well, maybe if I just stick with the lessons that he's teaching me, then I can learn how to be a rock star, because that was my ultimate goal as a kid. So ultimately, what ended up happening? I take all these lessons from him, learn how to play certain songs, and then I got to the point where I started maturing on my little music adventure. I was able to hear songs and literally pick them up by ear even more. It came more naturally, and I was able to pick up these songs. Of course, with Hector's help, I would ask him, "Hey, do you think you can teach me this song?" And then I start picking rock'n'roll songs and stuff like that. But he always wanted to keep me in that position to where I'm learning the flamenco or classical because those are the most complex of music. So as a grown man now I see what he was talking about, whereas as a kid I was like, no, you're full of crap. But he really just taught me the ways, so to speak.

I started taking lessons from him when I was a really young teenager. Because again, at that time, in the 80s, Metallica was just starting out. Being the rebel that I am, I was like, yeah, Metallica, cool. Anyway, that's what you know. It got me going in the music and I kind of ventured off into different things. Just watching my uncle growing up, playing different venues and just listening to him. How effortlessly he would play. There were times when I'd go to certain events and he'd be talking to me like carrying on a conversation while he's playing. I'd think, how the heck can you do that? So that always resonated with me as well. We had that relationship where we would always joke with each other and Hector's kind of a jokester anyway, and I'm kind of a sarcastic guy. So, we just gelled really well even as a young kid. It was just a fun time. Taking these lessons from him and realizing you know what his accomplishments were, even as a kid, because I'd see him play everywhere. I mean, this guy was everywhere. And I thought, wow, this is cool. I felt enamored, and I felt honored. It was just a cool feeling that I could just call Hector and say, hey, teach me a song and he can and he'll do that.

I have two Pimentel guitars. My father made me my own guitar. It's a grand concert. And then he made my son a guitar. And so I have my son's guitar in my house too because I just want to keep it safe. So every now and again, I'll pick up the guitar and I'll play. It's like riding a bike. You still remember the muscle memory, so to speak. And so I'll pick up the guitar now to remember some of the songs that Hectors taught me back in the day. I don't remember them. I would have to revisit the tablature and all that stuff, but I can. I remember the chords, the C chord, the D chord, the G chord and so on and so forth. So I still mess around every once in a while. Recently, I told Hector I'd really like to learn that Rolling Stones song, *Paint it Black*. It's rock'n'roll. He plays it all the time. I heard him playing it and I'm like, hey, I want to learn that song. So he started showing me. But again, you know, with my busy schedule, it's hard to come in consistently and be consistent with it and then go home and practice.

Back in the day when he had his group, what really drew me to his music was obviously the culture of of how we were raised and stuff like that. And it had that vibe of Latin music because most of the time he'd play flamenco. That's what he was known for at the time. He had a dancer and another guitarist. So that was kind of his genre and that's what really drew me to that type of music because, number one, it was my uncle and he played very well and I really wanted to learn that as well, along with rock'n'roll, of course. Rock'n'roll was my number one priority. But I also was drawn to that type of music as well. And so, when he had his group together, they would play at different venues. I was going and to me was just the most amazing thing. I talked to him recently. I said, Hector, why don't you get back into flamenco style music? I mean, he does do a lot of covers and stuff with the popular music. But I said, we're in New Mexico. I love that music. And he said, you know. I might start doing that again. You know, I might get my group together again. That to me was amazing and I think that people are drawn to that because we are in New Mexico. I feel like that's more of what people want to hear. You could throw in a couple of popular songs, but I think he has a knack for playing that type of music. It's automatic. It's like autopilot, the way his fingers move. The other night, when we were watching him play at Casa de Benavidez, you have to look to see how he's doing that. You're like, what the heck? How does he? How does he do that? It's mind blowing. I hear it because I know the guitar. I'm not a professional. Don't get me wrong. I don't play professionally. But I've played enough to know how difficult it is to do what he does. It's not easy. It's mind blowing because there are times when, depending on what the song is, you literally have to hit two or three strings at one time, and while you're holding a chord. So that it's not easy. You just have to practice. And if you have a knack for it, and if you have that natural capability, if you can hear music and you can translate that to picking up the guitar and potentially getting it down on the fretboard and the strings. I mean that it kind of all marries together.

So funny story. You'll probably laugh because I went from one extreme to the other. I was into rock'n'roll as a young kid and I've always been into music. So, as I grew a little bit older, more like a young man, I got into rap music. We were doing this kind of like Spanish rap, so to speak. We were promoting that type of genre. So one day we were

recording a song. And I was taking a couple of lessons here and there with Hector and I wanted to learn this one flamenco song, and he taught it to me. I can't remember the name of this song,. but I translated that to our recording session in the rap song that we were creating, and I actually played the guitar on that song, and it was just a quick snippet of that guitar riff. I guess you want to call it a loop. So again, I've always been in music, no matter what it was at the time, whatever's popular. I kind of just wanted to go after that. And then, of course, I grew a lot older, and I got out of the whole thing. And I said, OK, it's time to get a job. This ain't working out, but it was fun.

I've done a couple of things in the music industry as well. So I mean it's worked well. We did shows with Kid Frost or any of those big Latin rapper names like SPM, South Park Mexican. We did these big low rider car shows, and that was a cool experience. But because I wanted to do a song, and we were kind of the Latin group, I implemented one of the songs that he taught me into one of our songs. It was cool.

My son was learning as well, that's Robert the 3rd, and he did take a couple of lessons with Hector. My son is 26 years old. And he used to work here. But as a kid too, I also worked here at the shop. I tried it, but I don't think it was for me. Your heart has to be into it. You have to have a passion for it. And if you don't have a passion for what you do for a living, it just doesn't mix. I think that was the case with me. I wanted to, but I also needed to pay bills. They can only do so much for you here in terms of how much money they could pay you. But my son got a lot further than what I did in this business making guitars. When I was working here, I was the sweep up boy and the cleaning the bathroom guy. Then I would sand guitars and polish guitars. The way they teach apprentices over here is just the way they grew up learning. So it may not resonate with a younger generation, but to them, that was natural.

I think everybody's like this when you learn from certain people or certain teachers. If you're going to school or whatever, some of your teachers are like, oh, yeah, I get it. But then the next teacher, not so much. I picked up things here and there in the shop and they would try to teach me. I just got to the point where , well, I don't think this is for me and I think I need to move on. So I did. But now, sometimes, as an older man, I wish that I could have stuck with it a little bit longer, or tried a little bit harder.

My dad encouraged me to move on. Your parents want the best for you, no matter what you do. And I think the decision that I made was probably going to be best for both sides. You know what I mean? Because I remember sanding a hole in one of the sides of the guitars because I was going to town. I was being aggressive, sanding and sanding, and I looked and, oh, it was like a small, little hole. My dad wasn't too happy. That was one thing that resonated with me for a very long time.

And to this day, I'll talk to my dad about that same story. And I'll ask him if he remembers when I did that. How mad he was. Because that was an expensive guitar, and it was already built at the time. The sides were on and it was in its beginning stages. So when the back is on the guitar, you would have to put it in a vice and then you'd start sanding it and scraping it because you want to get all the imperfections out of the wood to make it straight and smooth. There's a process. Now that I'm older, I get it. But as a young kid, you just don't. You don't see it the same way. These guys, they were brought up with it.

I used to come here to the shop as a kid and this used to be a little tiny house, a little, tiny shack. I'd come in and I see my grandfather working away and then my dad would do his thing. And I was just a kid. I thought the place was huge. But it was a tiny little house. So they started expanding it throughout the years and it got bigger and bigger. But I just remember that my grandfather had ways that he taught his sons and you had to stick with it. You couldn't really branch off from that. You know what? It was the right way. So they were raised around it and they'd come to this shop as kids themselves. My dad and my uncles. That's just the way they were raised.

With Hector, you name it, he's done it. He's done events, he's done weddings, he's met presidents. And he's just done a lot in this industry. He's a staple in this town. A lot of people know who he is. Especially in this town. I wished he would have stuck with the genre, because I'm attracted to that music. I love when he plays the New Mexico flamenco style music. I asked Carol last week, "So why don't you guys play together?" and she said, "Well, right now he's mostly at the restaurant on Thursday and Friday. So we can't really do that inside."

She said they used to when they were outdoors. And I think there needs to be a certain restaurant that would support that. That's because it takes a little bit of room. And they did it outside at Casa de Benavidez and that was so cool because it just set the mood, it set the vibe. Of the whole restaurant. Again, you feel like when you're listening to his music, you feel like you're in another country, or like in Miami or something exotic, but you're just here in Albuquerque. You go there and you sit and listen to them and it takes you away.

I feel like with a New Mexico flamenco style of music, we are in New Mexico and most people gravitate to that. I've been talking to him about it. You've got to go back to that. It's just something that I want to see again.

So one thing I can attest to is you know when people take lessons from Hector is that they walk out of there and they start picking up on how to play the song. And when you have that situation, you build that confidence in that person. And so they want more. They learned something and they want more. Because they can do it now. Before they were scared of it, possibly. But he puts it in a way that makes you say, "OK, I get it now." I think that's what people gravitate to because when you can learn a song, and not have to worry about things like, do I have to learn the theory behind it? Not necessarily, you know. Like my son, too. The same thing when he took those lessons, he came out and my son has that knack for it. And Hector's kids. Like his daughter, Infania. Oh, my God, she just has that touch.

She picked it up like it was natural and even to this day, she'll come in here every once in a while and she'll pick up the guitar and Hector will say to her, play that song. She just picks it up and just the touch of how she plays it. She has that knack, too. She has that ability that people would die for. Because she grew up with her dad playing all the time in the house.

The funny thing is, when I was growing up, my dad didn't know a lick of guitar. Like, he didn't know how to play. He knows how to build you a beautiful instrument. Handcrafted. But he didn't know how to play it. Then, I don't know how many years ago, he decided to get Hector to teach him a

couple of songs and so my dad picked it up as well. And he plays, and he's pretty good. My uncle Rick thinks he can play, but I don't think he can. He's not very good. My dad picked it up pretty well, but Rick, he'll just kind of just drum notes and just play random stuff. Not even a song. Usually likes to test the guitars after he builds them but he just plays random stuff. I call it rubbish. Rick is Rick. My Uncle Victor actually started picking it up as well. So he's kind of picking up some notes and some certain things, but I think he's taking lessons from someone else. But he should. take lessons from Hector.

Hector just simplifies it all. That's the key. You simplify it and again, people can learn from that. Again, it's confidence. If you build up that confidence, then you think, oh, I can learn anything. Especially as a little kid. If you're a little kid and you're wanting to learn guitar and you know that there's theory behind it, you don't necessarily need that, and you can learn the tablature portion of it. Then you can learn how to play the music. Once you learn how to play the song, that's a confidence builder. Then you can probably dig into the theory later on, if you get serious about it. But I think for most kids, they just want to learn how to play. Get the guitar and then learn how to play a song. Hector's great at giving students that confidence.

Jaime Pimentel

Hector's Nephew

Hector is my uncle. My father was Augustine, Hector's brother. He passed away from a brain aneurysm. His brother Bobby, Robert, pretty much adopted me after that. He takes very good care of me and watches over me and gives me advice when I need it. He's always calling me and asking me, "How are you doing today?" He treats me like a son. It's really amazing.

I'm very fortunate, and even when I was a young man, and I went off and did my own thing. I was gone for quite a while. I raised my family, did a lot of things, had my children, and I was away for a long time, but I finally came back. I'm blessed to be a part of this right here. To have that kind of connection with everybody the way I do.

With Hector, we go back a long time. Even when I wasn't around the family too much, I used to go visit him over when he was playing at the Hilton and this guy always had a lot of amazing energy. He is really witty and just funny. I mean, he tells a lot of jokes. He's just fun to be around. He has a crazy personality, which just draws people in.

I used to go watch him play a lot of times and he didn't even know I was there watching him in the background. Sometimes I would go buy them a drink and be like, hey, I'm over here, uncle, because there's a crowd of so many people there. He'll go around the room and talk to you and sit down with you. That's really, really cool. He just has that energy. He'd buy drinks if he knew I was there. Guys will go talk to him, but a lot of females loved him. I was like, wow, you've got all these women after you all the time, you know, amazing. This is so cool. Some people just really admire him. I was one of those, especially when I was young and growing up, and I just saw everyone around him. He's a performer, and he doesn't slack on that at all. He's just really on it. He does know how to give an amazing show and really get out and talk to people.

People should go watch him play at Casa de Benavidez, especially when they're open for the summer outside. When it gets warm and they open up the patio area, he plays and it's really great to get out there. Go eat the good food over there and have some drinks. It's really cool just to watch him in action, especially if he has the band there. It's great seeing him play solo, but he has so much energy with the band as well. It's definitely really cool. I love to see that.

My kids, Mariah, Daniel and Kayla, are adults now, but Hector used to teach my kids how to play guitar when they were young. In fact, he taught two of my youngest, my son Daniel and my daughter Kayla. Daniel has a learning disability, so he had to come up with a new way to teach him how to play the guitar. It was amazing. He has a lot of patience and is an amazing teacher. I was so happy that he did that for my kids and they had a lot of fun. Hector had so much patience with them and took care of them. He didn't charge me anything. I was really lucky. He is dedicated to knowledge. He donated his knowledge and time and put a lot of effort into making sure my kids had a great experience with him. And I really did appreciate it. Trust me, I was like, oh, my God, my kids are going to get to learn something.

I think that one of my favorite stories about Hector is when I was going through a lot of hard times. I hadn't always kept a regular job. Especially after I got really sick and almost died. Never been the same after. I kind of lost my health a little bit. We were back in the shop and Hector was sitting with Pops, Robert. Hector asks me, "How are you doing this week?" And I was like, "I'm kind of broke, right? I'm not doing so well." Hector says to Robert, "You know what? I challenge you. Every time I give him something, I expect you to match

it." And you know, Robert went along with it. Hector's like, "Let's see what you got. I'm gonna give him a 20." Then my dad opens up his wallet as well. OK, boom. "I got you." And Hector says, "No, no, no, no. Do it again. That's not enough. Let's do another." And you know, that day I walked away with $200.00 and I really needed it. So that was really cool of Hector to kind of instigate that for me. It was just out of the kindness of both their hearts. That was really cool and a great thing. That happened right when I really needed it because I was hurting that time. That was really cool for them to be so generous with me. I've always loved them for all their generosity. They are real generous people with really big hearts.

You know, good people meet good people and everyone just clicks together and it makes life so much better for everyone involved, including everyone that's here in the shop. And you'll hear that just from about everyone that comes to the shop. I've met so many people from different countries that just come down to take a look and when they come to buy a guitar. Just to meet these good people is amazing. That's something that I've really enjoyed over the years is just being here, hanging out and getting to meet all these wonderful people that come over here. It's cool to see them interact with my family, when they meet Hector, when they meet Rick, when they meet Robert and Victor. It's really cool, just to see. How everyone just gets along so very well, and just to see that positive energy coming out. You can, if you choose, to come over and visit and say hi. You certainly are welcome and everyone's welcome over here. You come over here and come and hang out with us and have a good time. And it's just so fun being around it.

I do a lot of maintenance work like plumbing, electrical and landscaping. I'm really good with mechanics, like my uncles are wonderful with their hands. They do woodworking. I haven't really dabbled into woodworking, but I think that working with our hands comes with the blood. Even my grandpa from the other side of family, he was also a mechanic. You know my grandpa here was a luthier, and we are just really good with our hands. It's nice to get something done when you build something, to see it come from nothing to something, and it's amazing. It's a pride that my uncles have when they build these guitars, these wonderful pieces of art.

I've seen them buy wood and they've got large planks of wood. They can turn that plank into a whole guitar all by itself. Everything's handmade. They get a tree and make it into a guitar. That's not something that everyone could do. I've seen people, so-called builders. They have to pre-order a lot of parts already assembled and then they put it together and they call it handmade. But, no, it's not. My uncles, get the tree or wood that my grandpa had bought long ago and turn it into something that's handmade. Not too many people do that from scratch, like my family does.

They make it look really easy, but I'm sure that would be super hard. It'd be almost impossible for anyone else to do unless you've been doing it all your life. It's really cool to see that level of skill being put to use. It's like, wow, I watched them build guitars and they make it look so easy. It's like, "Oh my God,", especially when you see the finished product.

I'm sure that guitars were handmade at one time back in the old days, but nowadays it's all manufactured out. They don't have a soul like it used to, and it's sad that a lot of companies that make guitars have just lost that. It's amazing just to know that it's handmade and that came from someone's hard work and a lot of long hours. And that's important. You know that someone's heart and soul have gone into this. Blood, sweat and tears, like they say, and that's what it comes from.

The guitars sound so amazing. I think it's just because they've been improving, getting a better design after all these years. They keep coming up with new designs, making it better and better. So they sound better. They just didn't stop making changes to their designs, like all these other guitar makers have. When they started mass producing, they just stopped. And that's all my uncle's dad. They've been changing it forever. Changing it and making it better.

I'm very blessed to be part of this family and very lucky to be around all these wonderful people. And even meeting the wonderful people that do come in here. It's an amazing thing to even be just a little part of it, and I don't work here or do anything like that. But just this whole experience is amazing. I don't know what kind of person I'd be without it. It's really cool to think about that. Who would I be without this, without meeting all these amazing people or being part of my amazing family, and that kind of makes me think a little bit. And it's awesome to think that my life is so much better. With everyone in my life, friends, family, strangers coming off the street to look at these wonderful instruments, it's kind of jaw-dropping just to think of all the people that have been around and I've met out of all these years.

So it's really cool. And it's not only that: Hector, Rick, Robert, Victor, everyone, they're not only my family, but they're my best friends and not too many people could say that about their family.

Javier Serecerez

Friend and Student

I come from a musical family. My dad's a musician and my son's a musician. For some reason, that just skipped me all together. So I've been trying to catch up, I should say. And I've been taking classes with Hector for about a year now. So I'm trying to get back into it. I played a while a long time ago, but that was a long time ago. But that's how I met Hector. When my family was visiting from Las Cruces, we would go to eat at Ortega's. It was this restaurant that he used to play. It was a good place and I would go down there just to hear him play, and that's where we kind of just introduced ourselves. At that time, we would go there because my mom and dad would come up here just specifically to go hear him play. Ortega's was on Wyoming and Constitution.

In 2000, my father got really sick. He was in the hospital and I'd been meaning to buy him a guitar for such a long time. And that's when I came in here and I bought my dad a guitar. And so when he got out of the hospital, he had no idea. So we brought him up here and it was Robert that helped us to introduce the guitar to my dad. At that point, that's when I started hanging out with Hector

again. And, you know, we'd just kind of start talking about the old times and just kind of went off from there. And, the next thing you know, I'd be going over to his house and hanging out in his music room and playing music and then some of Carol's congas.

So we've been pretty really close in the past four or five years. I've known Hector for quite some time and he is an excellent performer. He's an excellent musician and I get astounded. I appreciate where I'm at in my life and within the Pimentel guitar spectrum because sometimes he'll go in the back and we'll sit there and we'll play and he'll be playing. And he'll be right next to me and his hands will be right here and you just you kind of stare. All this time that he's put into it. It's like, constant, nonstop practice.

When I first walked into the shop, I walked in and I heard him playing, but I didn't know it was him. I thought it was a Bose system. I'm like wow, they've got really good music here. This is really nice. And then it stopped and he started playing loud. Wait, that's that's not a CD! Who is that? And so that's when I found out he was up here. I appreciate who I'm hanging out with. And the talent that I'm hanging around with because it's not every day that you run into people like this and when you become friends and it's more of a family situation that you've got ties with. That's how I know Hector. And he's a great teacher. He really is. I mean, sometimes you have these really good guitar players or a really good baseball player, or basketball player, they try coaching and they just can't coach. I think he enjoys teaching more than he enjoys performing because it's like his knowledge that he's passing down. He's had a couple of students that are just remarkable. You can't tell whether it's him or.the students that are playing.

And then he also has some young people coming up and they're they're really, really good. And I was like, wow, he does well in both, teaching and performing. One thing that he drilled in me was practice. Your exercises. And that's basically what I what I've learned. We kind of go into music theory after that. And that's what I want to know because it's kind of hard trying to read the notes and play at the same time because there's so many things going on. But he makes it fun and he makes it nice.

I'm sure he's taken a lot of what he's learned and how he's been taught in the past has kind of pushed that through. He's been taught by some of the best from what I know, and just to have that opportunity to learn and to be given that.

So like I said, the whole generation of music just skipped me. But I'm here now. I get to go and hang out with the real musicians. It's a special person to be able to learn that language of music because it's a whole different language. It's like learning sign language. I'll sit there and say, well, what key is this? And he'll figure it out. Then he'll look at the strings and say, "Well, that's an E and that's an A. It's A flat." And then he'll tell you the chord I'm like. How do you do that? You know it so well. He'll start going into the theory there and I'm like, okay, I'm dying. I'm gonna go back and watch my television. I don't, but yeah. The thing is, he actually composes his own music. I mean, a lot of the stuff that you hear, he gets it and he writes his own. I mean, he writes the baseline, he writes the melody and the rest. He's really just one-of-a-kind. You can't make a cookie cutter of him, that's for sure.

William Loutfy

Friend and Student

I'm from Chicago originally, but I've been here since 1995, so half of my life here in Albuquerque, for all practical purposes. I'd seen him play at a restaurant, years and years ago. So I knew of the Pimentel name and I knew friends that had Pimentel guitars and had taken lessons. I crossed paths with Rick Pimentel and he said you need to start practicing. I was taking some lessons with another gentleman and I just didn't follow through.

Rick said, "You need to pick it back up again."

I said, "Wow, I suck. And plus, I get mad at myself."

He says, "I've got the best guitar teacher for you. My brother Hector."

And that was it. And he introduced me to Hector and he came in and I sat down with him. I had heard him play many times before. I just love Spanish guitar, it's so beautiful. It just moves you so much. And so I thought, well, I'll give it a try. I've been with him since October three years ago. But if you hear me play, you wouldn't think it's three years. It's challenging, but it's a good friendship and the brothers are all great guys. It's like coming to a frat house. They're like my frat brothers. They're really interesting and very, very funny.

Being a surgeon, I've been using my hand for over 30 years. I figured, I'd pick up a guitar and this is going to be kind of easy. But it's the most humbling, frustrating, piss-me-off experience that I've had. And he's so calm. I get mad at myself because I'm a type A and I want to do it right. And I can't get it right. I screw it up and he's like, it's OK. He teases me a little bit and he says you use your hands for a living and rolls his eyes, and pokes me a little bit. But, you know, it's just how frustrating it is for me knowing that I should try to do better and I'm having a hard time with it compared to what he's been through. To go back and recover and play seamlessly and beautifully. I guess that's why I look at myself like I should be playing better because I look at him and I think I should be doing this. I could just be using my hands and I didn't think to a step back and say, "Wait a second. You know, it's going to take me some time to be an expert." He's probably got 10,000 hours and he reinforces that with me. But

I just admire the fact that he would be able to bounce back and be that phenomenal to continue and not to have an issue with this.

What he described to me and knowing that mechanism of injury, I mean frankly, on a lot of levels, number one: he's lucky to be alive. Number two: not having some major neurological deficits and number three: to come back and play. Sometimes after head injuries, you have people that have personality changes or they are not as patient. He's extremely patient and I find that amazing because I'm not patient with myself and he brings me down to earth a little bit. OK. You know, you're not making career out of this. Don't try and be such so type A. So I really enjoyed the friendship with him and his brothers. It's been a good experience for me.

So I've been taking lessons for close to three years now. The challenging thing is with my schedule between my practice and just life, I have a hard time practicing when I should or missing appointments with my lessons and the like. It gets frustrating And when you don't pick it up for a while, then I get really more pissed off at myself and he's like, "It's OK, it's OK."

I'm going to be 64 tomorrow. And so with that in mind, I worry about neuroplasticity and using my brain. I think I'm pretty reasonable what I do for a career, but as long as I stay in my lane. But I think I need to really expand and keep my brain flowing. I don't want to be, you know, crapping in a nursing home. So, just like this, it's this neuroplasticity business. I think it's good to make you stop and think. Some days when I'm playing, I'm like OK, I think I can do this and I think it's going to be good for my brain. Other days, he must look at me thinking this is your first day, brother, you know? But I think just as a general statement, not just the emotional aspect of listening to music, but also just the better part of trying to keep my brain functioning. So keep something new and expanding my horizons, if you will. I love music. I operate three days or four days a week and I could operate without music, but it be pretty miserable. So we we play music in the operating room. I'm pretty eclectic. I play everything, Spanish guitar, old classic rock. I love the Rolling Stones. Pretty much everything. Bob Marley, Peter Tosh, the reggae stuff. The old rock, like the Eagles. He was working on Hotel California the other day when I walked in. He was really knocking it out. It was really cool. I just love music in general, but I guess just keeping my brain going and just doing something different. I tell you one thing when I'm here, I'm not thinking about work. So that's the thing, it's a good distraction. It's a really good distraction.

But you have to focus. Some days, like Wednesdays, it's a very long operative day for me and I come in Wednesday evening at 5:30 for a

lesson and I'm pretty burned out and I can tell. And I told him this and he picked up on it. The days that I've been working, when I'm operating, I'm not as tight. But Saturdays when I come here, I'm clear and I'm much more fluid. And he noticed that, too. He's, above all, just a phenomenal friend. He's a teacher. He's so patient. I'm clearly less patient with myself. And I get really pissed that I can't do something, and he's like "It's OK. Calm down." He's very patient and that's really very reassuring.

I took piano when I was a kid and it was miserable with an instructor with the conductor stick that would hit your fingers and stuff like that. Mr. Wilkins, you'll never forget that. You know it's impregnated in your brain like PTSD. But I was reading music as a kid, but I kind of put it out of my mind. And when I came here, I said, "You know, I was going to do tabs," and he goes, "Well, we could do that, but you need to learn to read music."

I said, "I'm in my 60s. I'm not going to read music. I can't do that." But he's got me reading music! So that's another neuroplasticity thing.

Hector is a living example of that, without a doubt, getting a a head injury like that. I'd be lucky just in general, but to have the neuroplasticity come back and play like nothing ever happened, that's phenomenal.

James Crabtree Sr.

Friend

I've known Hector for a long, long time. I'd honestly say he's one of my good friends. And I think I am to him, as well. My son is his student and my son fills in for him.

My grandmother was a classical pianist, so we were all supposed to be like that but I didn't. I'm the loser the group. My father, too. But not my son. He's Hector's student and even he fills in for him at Casa de Benavidez.

He started with classical music. He started when he was four or five. He was born in 1999. Vince Gill was popular at the time, so I got him a Tacoma guitar. They had a baby guitar out of mahogany, a beautiful guitar, and it's in the key of A. It's like a ukulele or those little mini Les Paul's. I got that for him just to make a statement and then he started playing it. We did the classical thing and I did that with him. And then I said, you've got to get a teacher. And again, Hector is the first thing in my mind. Boom, they hit it off. And the way Hector constructs the songs and his his vision of how to transcribe a song, like if it was a Beatles song, he's got that gift. And he makes it his own, which I don't know if people see that or not. I mean, oh, he's playing a Beatles song, not listening how he's doing the melody with the verses and how they've all been transposed together. That's him coming through. That's why I love Hector, because again, he's got that ability. Everything just comes to him and he's got that touch. It's just that touch. He's not stressing when he plays. It's from years of playing.

My son has a Pimentel guitar. Robert Pimentel made his guitar. The sound hole has a dreamcatcher on it. Hector's a fantastic teacher for him and it's like Hector taught him and then he's taken him for his own. I can't tell which ones is which when they play. He loves Hector to death.

Hector's definitely a staple of this town, part of history of this town. All through the 80s and 90s into into the 2000s. I tell him you should run for Mayor or Governor, because whenever something's happening, he's usually playing there.

Hector's playing is phenomenal, but so is his work ethic. I don't know if anybody's mentioned that, but his work ethic is amazing. It's one to be desired. I mean people don't realize he puts in a lot of hours. He's not only teaching, at which he's amazing, and taking the time, like with me or my son. He'll take the time to make sure whatever you're asking, he's confident in showing you because he has the knowledge of the instrument. And then he goes to a gig after teaching 7 or 8 students. I would be done with the 1st. He never misses his work. Never, unless you consider the accident. I'm sure he talked about his accident. I'd ask, "You're not going to go play?" He'd say "I'm gonna go play. I gotta play. I've signed and I can't not play." He's not doing it for the money. He's doing it because he committed to it. So again, his work ethic is bar none.

When he got his band back together, he brought the bass player back, the nicest guy. And he had Carol, his wife, doing percussion. I hope he does that again. And the dancers. Gotta have the dancers. And it seemed like they were doing a lot of that when Casa de Benavidez had the patio open.

My son, James, gigs, all well. He has Hector's work ethic, too. He played at VARA Winery for the summer. Highly recommended tasting room and winery right behind Balloon Fiesta Park off of Alameda. And I only found it because James got a gig there. We went and, oh, my goodness. The Paella is amazing. They don't have a kitchen but they have a food truck that cooks the food and brings it in to you They have a great wine selection, but they also do vodka, gin and brandy.

There's also Casa Rondeña winery. Hector's played there and I think James has too. I'm pretty sure they got a few gigs. It's competitive here for entertainers. James also played Vintage on Paseo del Norte and Wyoming. Highly recommend that one. Just get a hamburger there, though. Hamburgers are 21 bucks, but anything that you eat there is amazing.

When James gigged there, in fact, I laughed. It was so cute. Hector came with, Robert and Victor. They all came. They said we're buying the drinks and make sure you tip him. They all came to support James, but that was a big one, though, for my kid because it was a really classy joint. You know it's pricey, but it's a great. All of us out there just supporting him. And that lasted quite a while for the summer. James loved it. We got to meet a lot of local old musicians. I met the drummer from Sassy Jones. They were a band here in the 80s. They did the circuit. There was a club where they would pay bands to play and this was a great band called Sassy Jones. The drummer is still around. And he's teaching What? 1986 I saw you play and now you're watching my kid here? It's kind of cool.

We tease Hector on some of his gigs, like Little Anita's on Rio Grande and Lomas.. He did that one, I remember, and we liked it but I felt bad for him because nobody was coming in to that place except us. But I was like, oh good., it's quiet tonight. We can eat in peace and not worry. We teased him, but he played like the room was full. There was no one there, but he played.

James learned from Hector about performing and emphasized that with my son. You show up. You better be looking good. You're not wearing tennis shoes to a gig to play. You shine your shoes. You tuck in your shirt. You wear a vest. You comb your hair. That is huge. Be a showman. Hector is a performer. Some days, he probably feels like warmed over dog shit that day, but you know, he's ironed his shirt, shined his shoes, combed his hair, and put on the sunglasses. A lot of musicians or performers don't do that. But Hector's very high on that and I respect him for that.

Robert Pimentel, Jaime Pimentel, Hector and James Crabtree in the shop.

Rick Ambrose

Friend and Student

I grew up here in Albuquerque. I went to school here at St. Mary's from the 1st to the 12th grade. It's on Tajeras downtown and the school's still there. It was one of the oldest schools in Albuquerque. The oldest school is the Menaul School and then Albuquerque High School, and then St. Mary's was the 3rd oldest and believe it or not, my mother and father went there also.

I'm a Vietnam vet and I got drafted in 66. I got with Hector through his wife, Carol's sister, Becky. Becky passed away a year ago, but she and I were a couple and because I had met Becky, that's when I found that she was a member of the Pimentel family through her sister.

I had always dabbled with music in a way. I used to play the piano a long time ago. I played trumpet for six or seven years but got away from it. I thought, well, I'll come down and meet Hector and Robert and Victor and Rick. I had an old guitar. It wasn't classical, but I brought it down here to the shop. Rick said, you know, we can work on this, but he said it's kind of old. It was made so-so. I had picked that up somewhere. He said, have you ever thought about just getting a classical guitar? I said, you know, I never have. And he said, let me show you one of these. So he brought it out, and we sat down. And of course, I didn't play at all. He said, you know, my brother Hector, that's Becky's brother-in-law. And I said I'll be darn. And he said, why don't you take lessons? And this was over 15 years ago. So I started taking lessons. And when you start taking lessons, you want to purchase one of the Pimentel's because, to me, they are works of art. If you've been here before, you know what that is. And this place is very eclectic. And here they are like the elves working in the shop. I thought, wow, this is really something. So I started taking lessons from Hector, and I did purchase one of the guitars that was made by his dad way back, and it's a student model. I don't read music anymore and I thought, this is going to be a trip to try to get this stuff going, but at the time I needed something to do and I thought this would be a good opportunity for me. So I started taking lessons. And Hector is the type of instructor that's very patient, terribly patient. I'm fiddling around and I'm starting to get arthritis in my hands now, my right one, especially because I have a metal plate in here. I had an accident on an ATV. So it's sometimes difficult to pluck, but what I wanted to do was to learn to play somewhat classical flamenco style music on a guitar. We would come up here to this office and we just started off. Since I don't read music, Hector writes everything down on paper for the fingerings, for the frets, and I know a lot of tunes. And he said, what would you like to hear? I said, I love Guantanamera and I'm a big fan of Santana. One of his great songs, is Samba Pa Ti, which translates this song for you. So I was able to get some of that down, but it takes a progression of time and Hector, he says, don't worry about it. He says go slowly, always go slow. So for about 12,13 years, I've taken lessons from him. I still have the guitars at the house. I have a grand concert that I purchased. Rick and I did a trade, and so I have that at the house. A concert is much larger but is a beautiful guitar. And on top of that, it was purchased by a lady in Santa Fe who aged. And she came back here, and she returned it to Rick. Through all the years, they do keep a lot of their guitars that come back to them that are usually given back to them. He said, I want you to check this one out. So I did. And then, lo and behold, they refinished it, and they put my name up on the up on the top of the neck. And I'm thinking. Good God, I own a Pimentel and it's got my name on it.

They're a great family and I'm very fortunate to

know them and we've gone to many concerts. They used to have events at the Spanish Cultural Center and the Pimentels used to sponsor that all the time and now they would cover everything. They used to have meetings down at Gardunio's on Rio Grande in Old Town. And that's where I live. Just across the street. I would go down there and I'd never pay for a thing. They put on a spread. But they're a wonderful family. I know his mother, Hector's mom, and Gustavo. We've gone to many venues with them, but it's a wonderful thing as you get older. I'm 76 and to have friends like that and to be involved in some sort of music, it's a wonderful.

And I get emotional. This family has been through a lot. Hector's been through a hell of a lot. And for him to be able to continue with his music and his field after the accident he had, that's an amazing miracle. His ability to remember music, from memory, and to play Casa de Benavidez for years and other venues in town. It amazes me. My uncle was a classical pianist here in town. He's since passed. I took the piano from him for a couple of years. I couldn't remember it right now. When you get away, the thing with playing an instrument or being involved in music, you have to do it every day. You have to keep your hand in it, whatever it might be. Violin, oboe, stringed instrument, whatever it is. To keep your hand in it, because if you don't, you still remember, but the memory mechanics in order to play will go away from you. Like plucking, Hector is a great teacher for plucking. That's how he teaches his music for flamenco or classical. It's plucky, and I even grew my fingernails for a long time. Because the resonance of sound from the string on the guitar. It sounds much better when it's plucked with a fingernail than it is with a bare finger. And all musicians playing a string instrument know that. I didn't, and I used to always watch Hector, and he keeps his nails very hard. He must put a strengthening agent on it. You wouldn't want to get into a fight with him. Because he'd have, like, claws, but you can watch him when he's working. And that's a pleasure in itself. So I did that for a while and I'd hang out with different fellows off and on and they'd ask, "Rick, what are you doing with those fingernails?" I'd say, don't worry about it.

It's been a real thrill and a great opportunity to know them and they treat me like I'm one of the family. And it's because we keep in touch and I always come down here. Robert, when he's working here, he'll take a break, and he picks up a guitar. Rick also plays. I haven't heard Rick, except a couple of times. And Bobby's damn good and he'll pick out little tunes that we all know that we've all heard, and it's wonderful. So we just sit there and talk. He'll be picking away, and that's a pleasure in itself.

I guess the whole thing about it is having friends like this and being able to pick up a musical instrument like they have here, and it's always an honor for me. They even allow me to go into the workshop. It's kind of like a hall of fame or something, but just to allow you to be in there and watch them as they fabricate and each one has a certain thing that they do. Rick does mainly the inlays and stuff. I don't know how he does it and they come out beautiful and you're thinking somebody really made that by hand. To be a luthier. That's a lost art, and a lost profession, and for them to pick it up from their dad and to make this business what it is. They ship their artwork all over the world and they have a tremendous supply. Getting wood mainly from South America, which is very difficult to acquire now, but they have it stored and it just gets better as it ages and they work with it. The nice thing about it is when you have a guitar, especially, you can always go over, open up the lid of the guitar case, pull that thing out and it's like an old friend.

It's amazing that Hector writes his own music and he has to reverse it for me. He'd have his music out that he's playing the tune for me sometimes and then he'll get crossed up. And he'll say no, no, no, no. I got to put this here and so he'll write it while I sit right there. Then I take it home. And it takes me sometimes about two or three days, and that's spending at least an hour or two each day.

You have to spend time. You have to put your effort into it to get something out of it. But I know the tune. It's just me getting to that point when finally I'll reach that point and I'll go, Oh thank God, I finally got this song down. Yeah, I got the damn song down. And I'm good with it. And then I can remember it. And once you start, but you have to do it every day, then you remember and you don't have to look at the sheet music anymore, but it's memory and the response with your hands and position and all of those things. But I learned all of that through Hector. He's smooth as glass. He never gets upset. I've never seen him upset. And it's so easy.

Ben Perea
Friend, student, and music director

I feel like I've known Hector forever. I think I was in my senior year in high school, 1977. I didn't know what I was going to do . I had no idea what I was going to major in when I went to college. Then a friend of mine who was a classical guitarist said, "Why don't you consider something in music?" because I played guitar just off and on in a church choir and stuff like that, as a little kid. So I really never studied guitar. I said, "I don't know. I don't even read music." I learned everything by ear. He said, "Well, there are lots of teachers. Have you heard of Hector Pimentel?" I said I've heard of their guitars forever and he said why don't you take a few lessons and see what you think? I signed up with him right from the beginning, that was it. That's what I was going to do. He's exacting when he's teaching and he makes it look easy, like there's nothing to it. But when you're playing, he watches everything. I still tease him for yelling at me, for putting my thumb over the top of the neck. I started, and he taught me some real basic stuff and I said I kind of like this and I kept going for a couple of months and it was time to sign up for classes at UNM. He's the one that inspired me to keep on with music, and that's why I've been in music all my life since then. If I hadn't taken lessons from him, I have no idea what I would have done. I'd have still been playing guitar on the side somewhere, doing something, but not at this level at all. He took me from not even reading music and he's patient because most of his students probably know how to read music when they come in. Not even reading music to learning to read and play pretty complicated songs in a short period of time. He's a nice guy. He makes the lessons easy where there's no stress, no pressure. Once I started UNM, there was other teachers too, and it's like, oh, God, you dreaded going to that lesson because you knew that they're going to tear you apart for every little mistake and they'd point them out and want you to fix them right there.

So I've known him and his family and I've got several guitars made by them. They're one-of-a-kind guitars. I've got about 10 or 12 of them now. I know it's crazy. It's like an addiction. I started with just a Japanese-made classical guitar that I use when taking lessons from Hector. I opened the case one day, and the bridge had popped off. So that's when I had them build my first Pimentel Guitar. It's an amazing family and I like going to hear him play. I don't think people realize that he makes it look easy, but the level of music he's playing, he makes it look so effortless. You see him at the restaurant and he's not even thinking. I always sit there waiting for him to make a mistake just so I can tease him. Nope, it doesn't happen. It just does not happen.

He's just a natural musician, and he knows how to influence other people to enjoy the music that he likes to play. That's not always true with teachers. With certain teachers that sometimes you just don't want to be with. I always looked forward to coming to his lessons. You feel comfortable. If you make a mistake and it's like the same thing with some of the bands I play on, if some bands you make a mistake and they give you the stink eye. Like, what did you just do? Then there are some bands that say, well, no big deal. Fix it. And that's what Hector has that ability to do. If he wanted to, he could be another Andre Segovia that would just yell at you for the littlest thing. But he just points out what needs to be fixed, and it makes it fun. But he's that way just as a person too, always. You always feel like a friend when you walk in, not a customer. You always feel like a friend there. They are a very welcoming family.

Then I went to UNM, and I actually started majoring in guitar and I thought, I don't want to major in performance because anybody could perform. You don't need a degree to perform. So I went into music education and I became a band director. I taught out in Zuni for about 3 years, and then I taught at Valley High School for another 25 and retired from there. And all that is because of Hector. I'm not kidding you. And now I run a driving school. I don't know where that came from. I play just off and on, like at restaurants or weddings and funerals. I also play in a band called the Watermelon Mountain Jug Band. We've been around for 1000 years and a bluegrass band up in Santa Fe, and I play banjo and guitar with them, but the whole music thing started with Hector. And if my buddy hadn't recommended Hector, who knows where I'd be? I'd have done something, but it wouldn't have been my whole life.

Everybody knows Hector. If they ever ask me who I took classes from, I tell them Hector, Hector Pimentel. I've seen at performances like at the Kimo and the Hispanic Cultural Center where he had his whole band and that's amazing stuff, but he does amazing stuff just as a solo artist. I'd asked him, hey, Hector, I got to play a wedding. You know this song? Yeah, come on by. So I walk into his studio and he'll be writing stuff. I think he's taking notes or something like that. But he's writing out the arrangement while he's talking to me. Like, how do you do that? He'd be writing, and he'd be talking to me, but I thought he's busy.

But he said, here you go and hands me the arrangement. There's only been one other person that I know that could do. That was a banjo teacher I had, Wayne Shrubsall. And he would do that at the lessons. I finally realized he was writing down the tablature. He's like carrying a conversation like this. He's just writing it down, and I thought, OK, I can barely focus on the music and play. What's up with this?

I've been playing for a long time after I started playing classical guitar. Then I thought, you know this. I like the finger picking type stuff, but I didn't want to do. I do mostly finger picking guitar. And then I thought, what would be cool, banjo? Hee Haw was on television at the time and Roy Clark had a banjo player, Buck Trent. He passed away probably a couple of years ago. Buck Trent's son contacted me to ask me if they could fly me out to Nashville for a tribute to his dad because I played just like his dad. Well, that's where I learned, watching Hee Haw and Buck Trent. I asked him, how do you even hear about me in New Mexico? Not very many know about me. He said I saw your YouTube channel and you sound just like my dad. I thought that was pretty cool. And the finger picking stuff comes from Hector because he's exact. If you mess up one finger, he won't yell at you. He'll tell you, you know, it'd be better if you did a rest stroke here and that type of stuff, and that's when I transferred over to playing banjo. All

that stuff in my head, everything had to be exact, and that's what made it fall into place really easy.

I switched back and forth from guitar to banjo all the time now, but with all the finger patterns if you learn classical guitar, you can play any style. Everything is based on that from the left hand to the right hand. And it's important to do it the way he did it, I think because you can get a teacher that doesn't really play. One teacher at the university, when you go in for your lesson and his mind was somewhere else, and you knew you played something wrong. No problem. Just practice this one for next week. I didn't really learn anything, but with Hector, I said right from the beginning, he made sure that everything was established the right way from the beginning.

The guitar that had the broken bridge was actually a Hirade, a Japanese handmade guitar. It was a really nice guitar that I used up all through U&M, and like I said, I opened up the case one day and the bridges had come off. I thought I know the Pimentels do repair work, and I asked, Can you fix it?. And they said, Oh yeah, bring it by. And so they fixed it. And then I saw the guitars they have in here. I thought, oh, there's no comparison. And they're all custom made. So my second wife said that's all I talked about for about a week, and then she said, well, what style of guitar would you like? And I said, well, I think like a cutaway classical guitar would be nice. I didn't think anything of it, but she had them start building me a cutaway classical. That was my first one, then I said I need another. That's a steel string, so I kept on going. Now I've got one-of-a-kind. I think Victor called it a guitarlele. It's a guitar, but sound like a ukulele. I just had that made about four months and so I've got that.

I've got one that I had made for my dad after he passed away. Just in honor of him. And it's everything custom. It has the Air Force flag on the top and some personal items inlaid into the guitar of my dad's. Then I thought, how can I do that for my dad and not do it for my mom? So I had one made for my mom to call it the Celeste guitar with the Rose Vine and special memorabilia in the guitar itself and it was Brazilian rosewood. I try not to take it out of the case too much because, like, I'm not worthy.

I'd walk into the shop just to see what their latest things are. I ended up with a jazz fusion steel string. I think I've got about 10 Pimentel guitars. Another one that I got was the second state guitar. The first state guitar, I don't know what museum that's in now, but that I got to play it for the dedication and I thought I want one of these. They made me one, so I got the second state guitar. So it's really nice. And when they called me to do it, I thought, why are you calling me? There's a million other good guitarists around here. They said we really want you to. This is a steel string. You play

steel. So I got to dedicate the original state guitar for Hispanic Cultural Center. They had to get permission from the Zia Pueblo because they use the Zia emblem on it. It's a big deal.

Yeah, you can't stop because it's made especially for you. Like I said, they treat you like family when you walk in there. They're friends right away. And it's not fake. It's genuine. That's the kind of people. All of them. There's three different levels of the Pimentels. They have Hector sequestered up here for a reason. And then you go to Rick and he's the professional. The business end of the deal. Super nice and he knows everything. But once you pass that door that goes into the workshop area, now you've crossed into the dark side. Victor could be like the halfway point, but it's Robert, mostly in the shop.

Everything about the guitar, the bracing and construction, is their design. Everything. And it's all 100% handmade. I've been to the Taylor factory in San Diego, and it's really interesting, but everything's made with CNC machines. They're perfect. Every guitar is exactly the same. There are only a few little touches that the employees do by hand, but the rest is all CNC, and is just put in a clamp. The ones that are the top of line Taylors, the presentation series, compared to the material used in a Pimentel, you'll hear a huge difference. And I've got a Martin, a D45. Compared to the Pimentels, it's a way different sound. And if I had my choice, and this is not of which guitar I would buy, it would always be the Pimentels. I bought the others just because it's a cool thing to have. Trade in four guitars to get theirs.

I've played Pimentels a lot of times, but I play the state guitar when I play live. I take that one because the lead singer from the band always talks highly of them and I respect that, because he appreciates the guitar. Sometimes you'll play a guitar and people say, oh, it's really pretty, really nice. But when you take the Pimentel, you'll have a line of people waiting to see it at the end just to see it.

Paul Benavidez

Owner of Casa de Benavidez and Friend

We've been in business 43 years now. We started a little building across the street from the Alameda Post Office in the North Valley. It was a little shack, probably 300 square feet total. It was just a little carryout place. Now we're sitting on five acres at this location. I've got property all the way to the back. So we've been pretty lucky.

My mom and dad started the business. They got to that age where they didn't want to work for anybody else again. So they figured my dad would work in the back and my mom would work in the front and then make enough money to make a living. Within a year, it was going crazy. We only had like like 6 parking spots in the front and people were parking up and down the street.

So within two years, we found this building, and we moved into part of it just thinking we're going to be in the back part and we eventually used it all. The original house is in the middle of everything here. The right place at the right time, I guess. But when you grow up with nothing, you're very appreciative of your success.

I met Hector when he worked for us earlier in his career. I think he was here maybe a year. He was very young at the time. I can't remember how old he was. He never tells me his age, but I know he's a little older than what he says. I know that because I've had customers come in here and tell me we were in high school together in the 60s. So whatever. And I don't know what happened back in the day, but I guess he went on and he got other gigs and everything else. He started back here about 15 years ago now. It was right after he started to get better after the accident. And he finally told me that that's what helped him get along because he wasn't playing. I guess he was a little scared about going on stage anywhere. So we got him in here. It kind of got him back out and feeling good about himself. And like I said, he's got a lot of customers that come in here just to hear him, and then he gets little side gigs because they hire him to do other things. Yeah, he does everything. He's all over the place.

Matthew Martinez, the bartender here, calls him the banjo player. He'll say "The banjo player is here." But Hector's a really good person. We're happy to have him here, and I guess he'll be here until the day we close.

I had a friend of mine say find some other music and I said, well, you know what, I have a lot of customers that come in here just to listen to him and he brings friends and I and they sit there and they enjoy themselves like, why would I change it? It's like he's part of my family already. Sometimes you have a family that are not really close to you. And then you have people that end up being close. They are not blood, but they're still very close to you. Closer sometimes. And we shoot with the shit all the time. We give each other hell and he loves it. He'll say, "Why are you picking me all the time?" "You're picking on me, too." Just like he told me, he was shy when he came here. I told Hector, "You are never shy, so don't try to blame me." No, he's not shy. And if he's not shy because of me, well, I created a monster then.

I know all his brothers, too. I didn't meet his brothers until after he was here the second time and they'd come in here. There's one that I give him grief all the time, 'cause he just likes to pick on me, so I pick on him right back. All the rest of the guys are very nice, but Robert and I go back and forth. I told him once, I said, "Guess what, bro? Rick's not feeling too good. So I'm gonna leave the restaurant here, and I'm gonna be taking over his place, the guitar shop. And you're gonna be working for me." And he goes, "What? I don't think so." He said, "Rick said I'll be in charge of everything." Then he came over and he said I fired Paul over here and I fired Margie over here. So we go back and forth.

One time Hector was trying not to get so drunk but the customers like to buy him shots. So the waitress was putting the alcohol into a little glass to the side and giving him water. Because we're all doing shots with him, and if he was doing shots with all the customers, he wouldn't be able to crawl out of here. So they had a little thing going there to help him a little bit. It was Patron Silver, so it was easy to pass it off with water. So he was doing shots all night long and everybody thought they were doing shots right along with him and all he was just drinking water. They're all like we've been getting him loaded, and he's playing so well. How can he still play right?

I probably have more stories that I can't even remember. Every once in a while I hear an off-string and I go, oh, someone's had too much tequila tonight. But it's usually toward the end of the night. Well, it's hard to turn it down when the customers are trying to buy you something. That's kind of rude and I'm glad Hector's not a rude person. Most of the time.

Carol, his wife, comes all the time. She is the entourage. I remember at one time, he walks in and she's carrying all the heavy stuff. She brings the guitar, the amp, and he walks in here with nothing. Hector comes up to pick up his check from me and I ask, "Hector, are you going to help your wife?"

She's taking the congas in and all this stuff. Hector looks up at the monitor where the cameras around the restaurant are shown and he says, "I think she's almost done." Carol's great about it. But like I said, he was right. Watching the cameras, he goes, "Almost done." He's a rascal, and she knows it already. But Carol lets everything go off her shoulders.

Like I said, Hector is just good people and there's a lot of people that come out here to listen to him play.

Rita Benavidez, owner of Casa de Benavidez.

Richard Martinez

Friend and Media Consultant

I first came to the shop around 2005 or 2006. I had always heard of them and I knew of them and I played their guitars before. A friend of mine bought a guitar here, and that's when I met Robert. I was admiring the guitars and Robert asked if I'd be interested in getting one? I was like, yeah, but I can't afford it. Robert asked me what I was doing, and I told him I was going into the Guitar department at UNM, the University of New Mexico. I told him I couldn't afford it and then he showed me a guitar and said this one's for a really low price. A really, really low price. I said, alright, let's do it. So I went to the ATM to get the money, but Robert called me and said, "We can't sell you that guitar because Rick said it was the last guitar our dad made." I was so bummed. Then Robert said, well, we'll make you one. So then that's how I met the Pimentel's. But I'd met Hector a few years before that, from a friend of mine. My friend would frequent at the Ranchers Club and Hector would play at the Hilton over there. My friend was like, hey, you got to meet this guy, Hector. And I said I know who he is from around town. And so he put Hector on the phone and Hector said come hang out and you could even play, so bring your guitar. I never did. But he extended that olive branch, you know.

I was at the Community College at the time, but I was in a music school, and I was just maybe taking lessons, you know, starting. Fast forward, I came here and met Robert and Rick and had the guitar made. I started coming around more often, naturally, because I got a guitar made. And then I started taking lessons with Michael Chapdelaine. I got into his studio. He was the head of the Guitar department at UNM for many years. He was a real prominent teacher. So I was really proud of being there. These guys were really involved in my school career and then they made me another guitar, which Michael Chapdelaine didn't like. Later on I found out they had a little feud going on, not really a feud, but basically, Michael Chapdelaine wanted free Pimentel guitars and they didn't want to give them up. That's not to say negative things, but that's how it was. So I kept on coming around here to the shop. And then I decided to dual major. I was a music major with performance and then I was a Media Arts,

Cinematic arts the emphasis on cinema.

So I was doing the two so naturally, being with school projects and films. I would film them whatever I could and do videos for them. I'd film local fighters and celebrities outside of the music business, like Johnny Tapia, a local boxer. I did a lot of footage for his HBO movie. So I just started doing that, started playing music, doing music, scoring my own stuff. Having these guys give me musicians who used to score stuff. And then the Pimentel Concert Series, at the Hispanic Cultural Center, so I started filming them. I've filmed all their stuff. I'll be putting it on YouTube. All the little catalog of it. And so I did all that stuff and I got traction as a filmmaker.

And then I went into business for myself. I did a photography studio and then did videography and stuff, and I just became their media guy. So I do all their photos and whatever else they need done. That's how I decided to hang around here at the shop. And then seeing Hector more often and hanging out with him. We go see him play and I just got to know Hector, and then I would do his media. Hector is an interesting guy to work with. There's the big ego, but he's a good guy and we've bumped heads a couple of times, but we've always come out of it. He doesn't hold a grudge. We're always joking around and just messing with each other. Sometimes we'll ruffle each others feathers on purpose. That's because he's more like a brother to me.

Well, they're all brothers. I don't know how many brothers there are, seven or something. So you figure they're all competing for the same acceptance or whatever, right? You know, from mom and dad. So their egos are big. They beat each other up, but I'm sure if you mess with them, they'd all stick together. They are always a family. They've had their ups and downs. They've had their controversies but they're a strong, prominent family.

Being a guitar family, it's only natural that they'd spit out some musicians, like Hector, a classical guitarist. There's a symbiosis there, right? The symbiosis being that there's this prominent luthier family that makes these world class guitars that are not only famous in the state, but famous in the world. You have people come from all over. I've seen people come from Spain and Portugal and places like that. And the symbiosis is that they make these beautiful guitars and then he's a musician that gets to play them. It's the family and they all add to it, so it makes sense. How often, even in any other industry, let's say, a big corporation that pumps out a product, do you get the siblings and everyone in the family become a testimony of that product?

It's just sort of special like that and it's thick in New Mexico culture, Spanish, Mexican and New Mexican. They built the state guitar, just like the road runner is the state bird and the Piñon Pine is the state's tree. So that, that's cool.

So there's a lot of that and I get to be a part of it. They've taken me in. Robert is one of my best friends, if not my best friend. So I feel fortunate to know them and Hector.

That's what they exude to anyone that comes around. You know you feel part of something special. Like Hector, he's already established and you want to hear his flavor, his sound and get to know him. He's got a draw.

I met Hector a few years after his accident when I was doing his media. He gave me a lot of his medical records and pictures to see if we're going to use it on his bio or whatever. We never did anything with it, but that's quite a feat. For anyone to be in a traumatic accident and come back. That's another symbiosis. When the accident happened, the music probably pulled him out of it and gave him a purpose. I would imagine those pathways probably kept them from being depressed by doing something to focus in on a purpose, a higher purpose. I'm sure he's thought about it a lot. I think that tragedy helped Hector become better and maybe it knocked some sense into him.

As far as the guitars, I've got my fifth one being made right now. I even studied luthiers, and I made a couple of guitars myself. I studied with a guy with the gentleman by the name of Paul Hassan. But I immersed myself in the guitar. It's

why I'm here. I wanted to be a guitar player ever since I could remember. I just never had the opportunity. But I got older and had the confidence to say I'm going to go tackle it. So I studied with a few people. I got into UNM and studied Michael Chapdelaine. I currently, and for the last 15 years, have studied with John Truitt. He's a very prominent musician here. He was a teacher at the Academy. He retired from there, taught at UNM for jazz guitars. He studied flamenco guitar in Spain. He's a master flautist and saxophone player, and he's just wonderful. I still meet with him every Tuesday, like clockwork. So I know the guitar inside and out. At least I've tried to. Am I an expert? I don't know what that means for me. But it's become so prominent in my life that I'm best friends with the guy who makes my guitars and then I get to play all the stuff that I studied. I understand the world of guitars and know how magical it is. I'm very lucky to have the place here.

And then just to play their guitars. I've made them. I've played them. I've owned many of them. I'm sure anybody that's picked up one of their guitars will say that it makes you play better. When you get one, you'll understand there's something right off the bat. You just start playing better. Their guitars do not go out of tune. I can pull my guitar and it will be in tune. You could just leave it in the case and pull it out a year later and they'll still be in tune, I promise. You can't do that with a Gibson or Martin. Those guitars are machine made even though they say handmade. They're hand put-together but they run the necks and backs and sides on their precision machines. They put them together and they look great and they sound very bright. But the Pimentel guitars are hand filed and they're always touching and sounding and listening. It's got to feel like right. Robert just feels it and he has his own bracing pattern. All the other guitars are the same bracing pattern. They're very innovative. They have this honeycomb bracing pattern on my steel string and on one of my nylon string guitars. They're really thinking outside of the box here with respect to guitar. They are like the Stradivarius of guitars, if you ask me. The unfortunate thing about it is, there won't be these guitars forever, after the Pimentels are gone. All these guitars will be worth something. But the fortunate thing is, anyone that walks in here can be a part of it. And then they get to take lessons with Hector if they want. It's a magical, magical place. It's a magical family. Their dad did a good job. And how often do you know someone whose kids take over the business and not just do it better, but take the torch, run with it and make it brighter? So that's what you get here, this thing that's excellent. Their brilliance is that they're carrying on.

Victor Beserra

Friend, Percussionist and Bandmate

I met Hector years ago at the Hilton Hotel in Albuquerque. At the time, I was playing music with different groups, and I had seen Hector and his band playing this Nuevo Flamenco style of guitar. It wasn't traditional flamenco, but it was very catchy. It had nice grooves to it and things like that. So I happened to pull them aside and tell them that, you know, hey, percussionist and maybe you can use me one of these days. I think I can add to your music. He eventually called me. And that's how all this started. We started practicing and eventually he brought me on to the music scene with him. I knew of a bass player, Ray Avila, and I mentioned to Ray what was going on with Hector, so he came on board. He already knew Yolanda Lange, the dancer, because she and her husband would go to the restaurant, so I guess they got to know each other. Yolanda was not only a freestyle dancer, that's what I would call it because it wasn't traditional flamenco, but she was a freestyle type dancer with flamenco accents to her dance. She was also a very good seamstress. She designed all her dresses, really colorful dance dresses that she wore during those performances. And so we

started. She was a very intricate part of the group because people loved it. They'd never seen anything like that where a flamenco dancer would come out and dance to non traditional flamenco music. It had Latin rhythms to it. It had flamenco rhythms to it. It was very different. And that's what attracted people to come down and check us out. Plus, Yolanda had this charisma. She was able to grab the people and gain their attention and their confidence. She'd play her castanets and swirl around, showing off her beautiful dresses. I wouldn't say it was a gimmick, but it was a way to draw people into coming to see us. It was a nice performance. So we did that for years, playing at the Hilton.

We played every Friday and the crowds just started getting bigger and bigger and before we knew it, there were two to three hundred people in this small club. It was across from the Ranchers Club here in Albuquerque at the old Hilton, and it was called the Cantina. It was a happy hour establishment and the cool thing about it was that we got a lot of the UNM crowd. So a lot of young folks would come down and listen to music. They served chicken and beef fajitas and the pitchers of beer were like five bucks. So it was really a bargain. You got to eat. You got a great show. They loved it there. The crowds just started getting so big that they eventually put a pause on it because the people who were staying at the Hilton were getting disturbed by the all this music and all the crowds. They eventually started controlling the size of the crowds because there were just too many people. We played there for at least five years.

During that time, my cousin Rudy had just gotten an appointment to work for Coca-Cola. Before that, he worked for President Reagan. He worked as an aide in the White House. He gave tours and stuff like that. His older brother Frank was really active in politics and had gotten to know Senator Domenici at that time, who promoted Rudy to higher levels in the Reagan administration. When Rudy left there, he went to work for Coca-Cola. Coca-Cola had put him in a really nice position and finally had named him Vice President of Latin Affairs. His responsibility was to recruit businesses to invest in the Coca-Cola products, whether they were chain restaurants and things like that, but for the Latin community. It was in the early 90s that he actually put together a program at this national Republican Hispanic Caucus gala, so he was a part of it because Coca-Cola sponsored it. He was very

instrumental in getting talent for the gala and he wanted to showcase New Mexican bands, so he asked if we would play for it. So we did. It was a reception prior to the Selena major concert. The way Selena got into the picture was Rudy had already had talks with her to be the spokesperson for Coca-Cola at that time because they were getting different stars and she was up and coming. She was young and a new face. And so they had already signed her up for a contract with Coca-Cola to be their spokesperson for Latin Affairs. She had been recording her music, Tex Mex music and Mexican, in Mexico and other places, but this was the first crossover album that she put out and was ready to release it. And so during that time in the early 90s, Coca-Cola flew us to Washington, DC and put us up at the Ritz Carlton. We played for the reception prior to the concert where Selena was performing. I met Selena backstage. I had heard of her, but I didn't really know the music. So she explained it to me and she was really, really kind and nice about it. She was a young girl. And she was a hit. The whole thing was a hit. We enjoyed our stay there. They treated us like rock stars, which was pretty cool. But the experience was very, very overwhelming. Sometimes when I think about it, it was because they picked us up in a limo and they drove us to the Ritz Carlton and the whole process. The doorman comes out; they open up the door of the car and you've got to give them some money. And then you go to the steps and they grab your luggage and you give them more money. And you're two or three hundred dollars in the hole and you haven't even gone to your room yet. Rock stars except with a beer budget.

We did some other things with the Coca-Cola. They weren't quite as big. Actually, my other cousin, his older brother Frank, worked for a media agency in Miami and they were doing things in Texas. They did this huge concert in Houston and they asked if we would be willing to perform at that concert, which we did. We actually did open up for Malo at that time. But this was, of course, a little later than that. And there were a lot of different Latin stars that were on that program. Coca-Cola was really good to us at that time. So we did some really major concerts during that period.

But I've been playing with Hector on and off for years. He'll just call me and ask, "You want to play with me?" Yeah, let's go. I played with him at quite a few different venues. The one venue that I'm sure he's talked about is when we played at the UNM Library. We were parking our vehicles, and they had this gate that slid on a track, kind of like a barn door track. And it was huge. It was probably a four or five hundred pound gate. Apparently, they were having issues with it and they didn't tell us what those issues were. But Hector went to

close it because he was the last one out and the gate came off the railing and fell on him. And that was a whole different thing that changed him. It changed his perspective on life. He had a lot of attempts to get back into the music, but he couldn't remember things. So that took a lot of time. He's doing a lot better now, obviously. But that was a very scary night.

After he recovered, I played with him at Casa de Benavidez for probably two or three years. We were playing outside during the summer months and then during the winter months, they'd take it inside. It was just too loud for the patrons that were there. So we kind of disbanded that, since he solos there. He has a bass player that sits in every once in a while and, of course, Carol does her thing.

He's been really good. Carol's been really good. They obviously have a good relationship and that's what really settled his lifestyle. She's very patient and understands him and knows what his moods are.

He's a fantastic artist. He's got a lot of skills that I like. To watch his finger picking is very, very impressive. And so I play with him whenever he calls me. When he mentioned that you were doing this book, I was really glad to hear it. I think he does have a story to tell. Like some of the times that we were playing at the Hilton where the women would get up on top of our PA systems and they were dancing and doing all kinds of crazy things. It was an experience, but it was enjoyable when everybody seemed to have a good time. That was definitely the place to be every Friday. I had a lot of friends that would go down to see us and they tell me, "Vic, reserve us some tables." So I'd reserve two or three tables. And sure enough, they did fill up. It was a really exciting and motivating type of environment. They literally had conga lines going around the tables. It was just great. In fact, we drank a lot of beer. The crowd was buying all the pitchers, and we were drinking that stuff like water, you know? We tried to maintain some sobriety.

So we had a very interesting and sometimes challenging time. He went through a lot. I witnessed a lot of his trials and tribulations. And I just kind of went with the flow. One of the things I admire about Hector is that he's a workaholic. He does not miss gigs or anything. He's always there, sick, no matter what, he's always there. He's got a really incredible work ethic. So that's kind of admirable for me. He kind of held this together a lot of times. I used to hate to come to rehearsal and but we rehearsed probably twice a week. And so right here, it was very easy. These were very exciting moments in my life that I'm glad I lived through them.

I eventually got out and did some other work with different groups. I played pop music. I played some tributes to The Allman Brothers. We did that most recently and just a lot of different genres, just so I could get a feel for that style. Just because you're a Latin percussionist doesn't mean that you're tied into one style of music. So I wanted to learn big band. I wanted to learn jazz. I wanted to learn salsa. I wanted to learn Latin jazz. I learned all these different types of music that would give me a better understanding and tell folks, yeah, I can do that. I can play that music and I've done it, so that helped me out a lot. I have congas. I've got bongos. I've got timbales, cymbals, chimes, all that stuff. I've got a big setup of stuff. I did the Latin percussion music without a drummer. I did that for almost the entire time that we were together. We didn't have a drummer, so I had to bring all this stuff and kind of fill in where I could. That was a unique sound. It's a unique sound that you don't hear everywhere. I really liked that. Hector just wants to keep playing, wants to keep doing his thing, and I encourage that. And I want to do it with him.

At one point, they were going to build a stage for us at Casa de Benavidez. Paul told us that he was going to build a stage because we had that little tent. When it rained or got windy, we had a lot of issues, so he said he was going to do that, but it never happened. Everything changed because of the pandemic.

I was playing with a gentleman by the name of Franc Chewiwie. He's from New Mexico and he's a Native American. His ancestry anyway. He plays the piano. He's does a style of Latin music that is kind of his own creation. He's written several songs. There are several tunes recorded on a heck of a lot of different albums. I've recorded with him on several of them as well. He's 90 years old now. He was playing, and I'm not kidding you, at the Golden Corral on Coors Blvd and Quail Rd. He was doing a solo gig over there, just playing piano and then he called a couple of his musician friends to come and help him out. So they started coming around and helping him out. It didn't pay very much. Before you know it, he starts calling me and says, "Vic, can you come down and play a little conga for me over here?" He's a good friend of mine, so I was willing to help him out. So we started getting this group together. We had Franc, we had Ray Avila, we had Pete on drums and David Nunez on guitar, vocals, piano, and you name it, he played everything. And we had Sel Garcia, who played saxophone. The sound was incredible. And for us not rehearsing, these guys are veterans. You know, it didn't take much. It's like riding a bike. They call out a song, and they all know it. So it turned into a big thing.

During that time, Franc was working with another vocalist. His name was Josh and Josh was from Mexico, but he was living in the United States. I think he had polio when he was a kid. But he was an incredible musician. He wrote his own music. He played guitar, he could sing. He was a really, really talented individual. And I played with him together with another guy because I wanted to capture the uniqueness of the music because it was kind of like Hector. It was a whole lot different. You just didn't hear it. So we did some stuff, but I left that group because of some other issues, but Josh stayed around and, I don't know how this happened, but Franc hooked up with him along the way and Josh ended up moving into Franc's home, so he was there and they were playing music. Josh then rewrote some of Franc's music and sung it. He wrote the music arrangements differently and sung it differently. It came out really cool, really, really cool. So Franc sent it to Sony and Sony called him back and said we like the music. We want to do something with you and they sent him a contract. They flew him out to New York, which is where he is at this moment. And they're recording his music. He wanted to take his band with him, us, but Sony said no, this is just you. We've got a thousand studio musicians over here that will do. So that's what they're doing. He got this five-year contract to play music, do some concerts, do whatever. So that's what he's doing at 90 years old. That is incredible.

So now we're with Hector here. We're going to make it good if we can get the right combination of talent. I don't know if he has a dancer or not. I think that's the key. His music is obviously very good. The style that we play, it works with the music, but it's that one dancer that can stimulate the crowd and that's the gimmick. To do something different. Doing something different that the people love, especially the older crowd that doesn't get to see the kind of music that they remember. They see the mariachis and maybe they'll see the flamenco dancer here and there but they don't see it on a scale where there is Hector's sound and the Latin percussion sound, and of course the bass adds a lot to the music, but the dancer seems to really get the crowd going. So I'm looking forward to it.

Carol, Hector and Victor Beserra

Hector, Victor Beserra and James Crabtree Jr.

Infania, Rachael, John with Daddy Hector near Old Town ABQ

Family

Hector's mother, Josefina Pimentel

Hector and Carol on their Las Vegas honeymoon.

Rachael, Carol, Mari (Hector's sister), Josefina, Ida (Hector's sister) and Infania.

Hector and son, John.

Daughters Rachael and Infania

Hector's sister Zoyla and her husband George

Hector and Carol with some much needed down time at the casino

Son John and Hector at Main Event

Husband and wife performers, Carol and Hector at a Christmas Party

Master guitar builders Victor, Robert and Rick

Rachael, Isaiah, Hector and Infania

Hector's Christmas Story

Too much eggnog, Hector?

Hector Pimentel and Hillary Smith featured on the cover of Albuquerque The Magazine, September 2017 issue.

Honors and Awards

OFFICE OF ANTITERRORISM ASSISTANCE
BUREAU OF DIPLOMATIC SECURITY
U. S. DEPARTMENT OF STATE

HECTOR PIMENTEL

IN RECOGNITION OF YOUR OUTSTANDING
CONTRIBUTIONS TO THE MISSION OF THE OFFICE OF
ANTITERRORISM ASSISTANCE,
AND WITH SINCERE APPRECIATION FOR YOUR SUPPORT
TO THE ALBUQUERQUE ATA TRAINING CENTER.

YOUR MUSIC HAS ENTERTAINED COUNTLESS FOREIGN
POLICE DELEGATIONS AND THROUGH YOUR EFFORTS,
THE MUSICAL TRADITIONS OF THE SOUTHWESTERN
UNITED STATES HAVE BEEN CARRIED TO MANY
CORNERS OF THE WORLD

FROM

THE STAFF AND MANAGEMENT OF THE
OFFICE OF ANTITERRORISM ASSISTANCE

DECEMBER 2001

Hector with First Responders in December, 2001.

Campaign 2001

This Certificate of Appreciation is Bestowed Upon

Hector Pimentel

For Dedicated Volunteerism,
Great Enthusiasm,
Tenacious Loyalty and Devotion to Task.

You Are the Best!

Martin J. Chávez
Mayor Elect

Margaret Aragón de Chávez
First Lady Elect

"Infania" - 1996 New Mexico "MIC Award for Best Song Guitar Instrumental

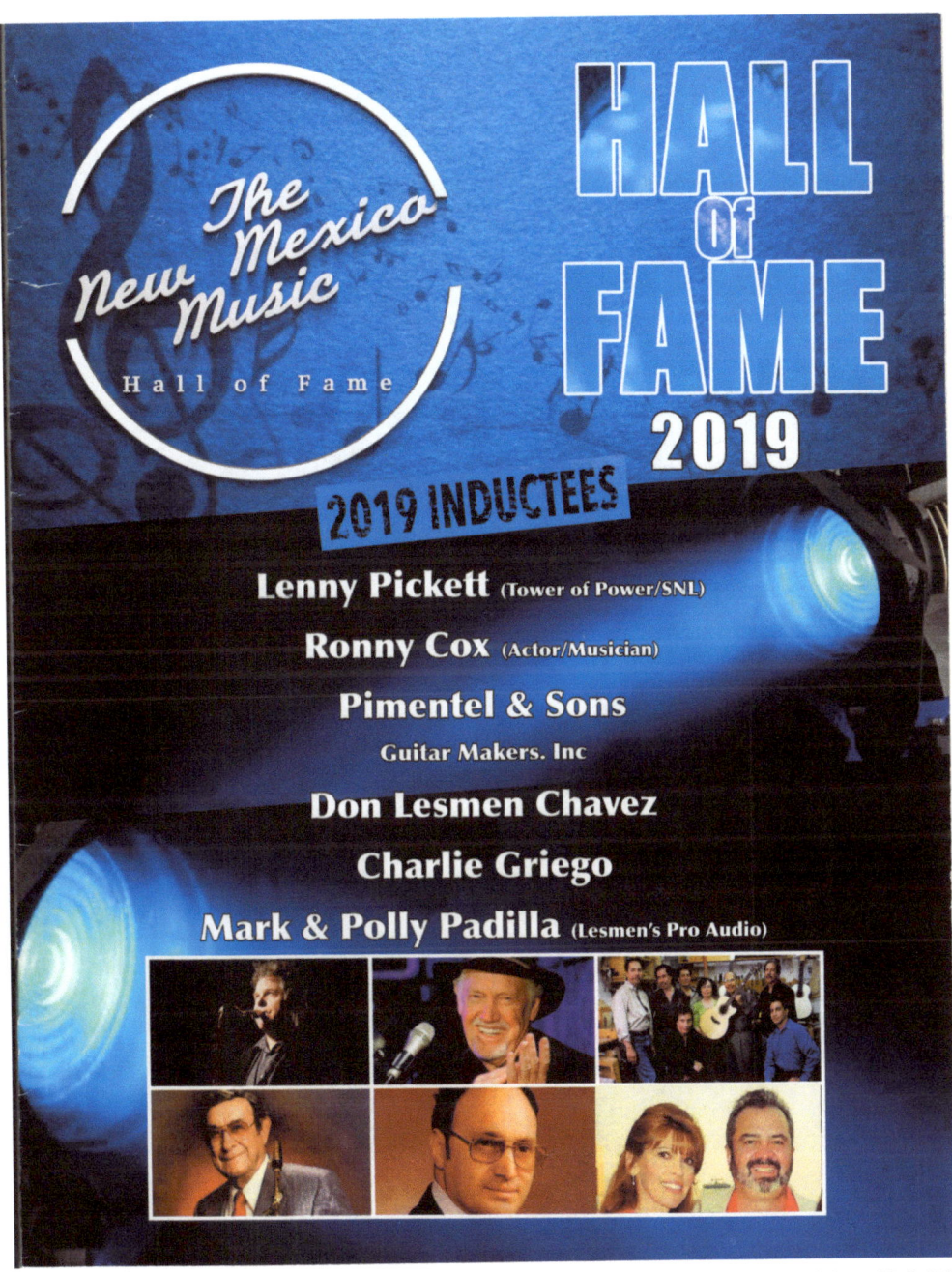

The Pimentel Family as Pimentel & Sons Guitar Makers, Inc. inducted into the New Mexico Music Hall Of Fame

Performance in Houston, Texas with fellow performers.

Hector's Scrapbook

Fans, Fun and Celebrities

Hector with Beau Bridges and Daniel Sonis.

Hector with New Mexico politician Steve Pearce.

Ana Vidovic, classical concert guitar artist with Hector.

Ed Romero, Ambassador to Spain, and Hector

Hector and Don Edwards, former director of the Balloon Fiesta at Casa de Benavidez

Hector and Ricardo Pacheco violinist at the
Spencer Theater in Ruidoso

Madison, one of Hector's students, with Hector
at Casa de Benavidez

Joe Diaz (meteorologist) and Hector at Casa de Benavidez

Daniel Sonis, (unknown) American Ninja Warrior, Hector, Vincent Hernandez

Always more fans.

Hector and Edgar Cruz, a guitarist from Oklahoma.

Hector Pimentel & Leyenda
INFANTA

Hector Pimentel   Passionate Heart

HECTOR PIMENTEL & LEYENDA
MASTERPIECE "ALMA LATINA"

Hector Pimentel & Leyenda
Smile Like A Billionaire

Discography

Infania

Nuevo Flamenco Music
©1995 Hector Pimentel. All Rights Reserved

Infania..Hector Pimentel
Cuando Caliente El Sol ....Carlos Rigual
Fuego ....Hector Pimental
Memories From Afar ....Ambrose Rivera
Barcelona Nights...Ottmar Liebert
Y Volvere...Alain Barriere
La Gitana..Hector Pimentel
Malaguena En Fuego ....Eresto Lucuona
Romance Of Love..Anonymous
Sambita..Ambrose Rivera
Samboleo ....Ambrose Rivera

Passionate Heart

Dust In The Wind
Lagrima (Tears)
Cherry Pink, Apple Blossom White
Romance De Amor
Cuando Caliente El Sol
La Virgin De La Macarena
Stairway To Heaven
El Condor Pasa
Adelita
You Don't Send Me Flowers Anymore
Passionate Heart
Granada

Masterpiece "Alma Latina"

If I Were A Rich Man ....J. Bock
Don't Cry For Me Argentina ....A.L. Webber
Samba Pa Ti / Europa ....Carlos Santana
Have You Ever Really Loved A Woman.........................Bryan Adams
My Way ....P. Anka
Never On Sunday ....Towne - Hadjidatis
Sabor A Mi...A. Carrillo
Can't Help Fallin' In Love With You ....Marini-Weiss
Con Los Años Que Me Quedan ....G. Estefan
Music Of The Night ....A.L. Webber
Solamente Una Vez...A. Lara - R. Gilbert
What A Wonderful World .... L. Armstrong

Smile Like A Billionaire

Pop Crossover Music
©2010 Hector Pimentel. All Rights Reserved.

By The Time I Get To Phoenix ....Jimmy Webb
Billionaire .... Travis McCoy
Here Comes The Sun... The Beatles
El Farol..Carlos Santana
Folsom Prison Blues .... Johnny Cash
A Day In The Life Of A Fool (Black Orphous) ....Luiz Bonfa
I Walk The Line... Johnny Cash
My Way .... Paul Anka
Caravan..Duke Ellington
Smile.. Chalie Chaplin
My Girl... The Temptations
Music To Watch Girls By ....Al Hirt

163

Merry Christmas From Hector Pimentel

Christmas Arrangements
©2010 Hector Pimentel. All Rights Reserved

Jingle Bell Rock
We Wish You a Merry Christmas
Away in a Manger
Jingle Bells
Blue Christmas
Silent Night
O Come All Ye Faithful
Silver Bells
What Child Is This
O Little Town of Bethlehem
White Christmas

Desert Wind Press Publisher,
Robert Brent Gardner

From the Publisher and Editor

Robert Brent Gardner

I first encountered Hector Pimentel, like many people encounter him, at Casa de Benavidez Restaurant on Fourth Street NW in Albuquerque. It was 2016 or 2017 and my wife, Rebecca, and I were new to the area, recently having moved from the Midwest. We were sitting at the bar and Matthew, the bartender, convinced Rebecca to get an egg on top of her "Old Fashioned" (the entrée, not the drink). I ordered Carne Adovada, daring to try the Red sauce. We listened and watched Hector play while we ate what we thought was the hottest food on the planet. Alas, we are gringos and were new New Mexicans. But I was entranced with Hector's playing. Both hands moving like a concert pianist on a gorgeous classical guitar. But we decided not to go back because we thought the food was too hot.

Fast forward to the post-pandemic era, and after a few years of getting used to the heat of the state question, "Red or Green", we headed back to Casa de Benavidez, and Hector was still there. We enjoyed his playing so much we would drag our neighbor, Beverly Ledbetter, with us. I had published two of her books in the past, and one of

her late husband's. One of her books covered her time in the foreign service. She had spent time in Portugal during one of her posts and learned to love Spanish guitar. She even bought a Spanish guitar and took some lessons during those days, but, alas, you have to keep your fingernails trimmed on your left hand, a non-starter for most women.

Hector's sets are about an hour long at the restaurant, then he works the crowd, like all good performers do. He would come to our table and Beverly would request various classical guitar songs that Hector, of course, knew. He would woo her with "Romance of Love", then break into "Malaguena En Fuego", much to the chagrin of the staff at Casa de Benavidez. "Too loud!" they'd tell Hector.

One evening, he spent more than the usual time with us at our table. He basically told us his life story, including the terrible accident that befell him. Hearing what he had gone through and how he's overcome so much, Beverly looked at me and said, "He needs a book!" and Rebecca and I wholeheartedly agreed.

Knowing that Hector would probably never sit down and type out his story, I tried to make it easy on him. I decided to record conversations with him, then transcribe them into text. So, from the middle of August 2024 to the end of May 2025 we recorded sessions on an almost weekly basis, outside of holidays and illness that took us over at the end of 2024. This book is the distillation of those sessions. We would trigger Hector's amazing memory as we went through the sessions, remarkable after such injuries. The words herein are Hector's and the other contributors that I recorded at Hector's request.

As I listened to the contributors, including his brothers that make the most fabulous guitars in the world, to his students, to his friends, and to his children, I came away with a feeling of being very fortunate to gaze into this close, extended family. They all spoke of Hector's kindness, patience, generosity, ability, but most of all, his love of music. He gives that love to students, to his audience and to anyone who wants to listen. Hector and the Pimentel and Sons family of guitar makers are indeed a New Mexico treasure.

Hector with Beverly Ledbetter, the instigator of this book.

Hector is available for:

Lessons

Weddings

Private Parties

Corporate Events

Contact Robert Pimentel

(505) 884-1669

info@pimentelguitars.com

www.pimentelguitars.com

www.ingramcontent.com/pod-product-compliance
Lightning Source LLC
Chambersburg PA
CBHW041426120626
46547CB00002B/111